TIMELESS WISDOM
ON

Prayer

T0017883

TIMELESS WISDOM
ON
Prayer

COMPILED BY
WARREN W. WIERSBE

KREGEL
CLASSICS

Timeless Wisdom on Prayer
compiled by Warren W. Wiersbe

Published by Kregel Publications, a division of Kregel Inc.,
2450 Oak Industrial Dr. NE, Grand Rapids, MI 49505. All
rights reserved.

Previously published as *Classic Sermons on Prayer.*

Library of Congress Cataloging-in-Publication Data
Classic Sermons on Prayer/ compiled by Warren W. Wiersbe.
p.cm.-{Kregel classic sermons series) Includes biographical
references and index.
1.Prayer-Sermons. 2. Sermons, English. I. Wiersbe, Warren.
II. Series.
BV213.C49   1987   248.3'dc20   87-3104

ISBN 978-0-8254-4854-6

CONTENTS

PREFACE

This series is an attempt to assemble and publish meaningful sermons from master preachers about significant themes.

These are *sermons*, not essays or chapters taken from books about themes. Not all of these sermons could be called "great," but all of them are *meaningful*. They apply the truths of the Bible to the needs of the human heart, which is something that all effective preaching must do.

While some are better known than others, all of the preachers, whose sermons I have selected, had important ministries and were highly respected in their day. The fact that a sermon is included in this volume does not mean that either the compiler or the publisher agrees with or endorses everything that the man did, preached, or wrote. The sermon is here because it has a valued contribution to make.

These are sermons about *significant* themes. The pulpit is no place to play with trivia. The preacher has thirty minutes in which to help mend broken hearts, change defeated lives, and save lost souls; and he can never accomplish this demanding ministry by distributing homiletical tidbits. In these difficult days, we do not need "clever" pulpiteers who discuss the times; we need dedicated ambassadors who will preach the eternities.

The reading of these sermons can enrich your own spiritual life. The studying of them can enrich your own skills as an interpreter and expounder of God's truth. However God uses these sermons in your own life and ministry, my prayer is that His Church around the world will be encouraged and strengthened.

WARREN W. WIERSBE

The Word That Conquers God

Clarence Edward Noble Macartney
(1879-1957) ministered in Paterson, N.J., and
Philadelphia, PA, before assuming the influential
pastorate of First Presbyterian Church,
Pittsburgh, PA, where he ministered for twenty-
seven years. His preaching especially attracted
men, not only to the Sunday services but also to
his popular Tuesday noon luncheons. He was
gifted in dealing with Bible biographies, and, in
this respect, has well been called "the American
Alexander Whyte." Much of his preaching was
topical-textual, but it was always biblical,
doctrinal and practical. Perhaps his most famous
sermon is "Come Before Winter." The sermon I
have selected is taken from *The Greatest Words in
the Bible and in Human Speech*, published 1938
by Cokesbury Press.

Clarence Edward Macartney

1

THE WORD THAT CONQUERS GOD

WHAT MIGHTY word is that? What word is so mighty that it can conquer God? What is the word that turns captivity captive? What is the word that unites far separated souls around one common mercy seat? What is the word that brings man's storm-driven ship into the haven of safety and peace? What is the word that turns back the shadow of death on the face of life's dial? What is the word that gives songs in the night and that lifts the load of guilt from the conscience-smitten heart? What is the word that puts a sword in our hand when we face temptation? What is the word that gives us strength to bear our daily burdens? What is the word that fortifies the soul when it kneels before its cup in some Gethsemane of sore agony? What is the word that lifts us up when we have fallen? What is the word that brings angels down from heaven to minister to us when we have overcome the devil? What is the word that makes us co-workers with God in the coming of His kingdom? What is the word that recalls the wanderer from the far country? What is the word that is the best physician for both body and soul?

What is the word which, when we speak it, may set a captive free? What is the word that companions the soul in its hours of loneliness and that comforts it in the day of sorrow? What is the word that sets a lamp of forgiveness and reconciliation in the window for the prodigal and the wanderer? What is the word that brings the eternal world to view? What is the word that is the simplest form of speech that infant lips can try? What is the word that is the sublimest strain that can reach the majesty on high? What is the word that makes the angels rejoice when they hear it on the lips of a contrite sinner? What is the word that is our watchword at the gate of death, the word with which we enter heaven?

That mighty, all prevailing, God-conquering word is prayer. *"The effectual fervent prayer of a righteous man availeth much"* (James 5:16).

The word that conquers God! That is a bold thing to say, and yet we say it by the authority of none other than the greatest example in prayer, our savior Jesus Christ, who said, "Knock and it shall be opened unto you," and who told two parables, the parable of the Midnight Visitor and the parable of the Widow and the Unjust Judge, to encourage us in prayer and to show how prayer conquers God.

When we come to select examples and illustrations from the Bible which prove and demonstrate our proposition that *prayer* is the word that conquers God, our only embarrassment is the riches of the Bible in that respect, and our only difficulty is to decide what instances of God-conquering prayer to select.

Abraham's Prayer

We commence with the first recorded prayer in the Bible (Genesis 18:23-33), the prayer of Abraham for Sodom and Gomorrah. It is a striking and beautiful fact that in the Bible, which is the great treasury of prayers, the first recorded prayer—is a prayer of intercession. There prayer is seen at its highest. Life's golden altar is the altar of intercession. A person never does a nobler act than when he becomes a priest to others and makes intercession for them.

As Abraham sat before his tent on the plains of Mamre, he lifted up his eyes, and lo, three men stood by him. After the men had been graciously entertained by Abraham, they gave him and his wife Sarah the promise that a son would be born unto them. Then they departed in the direction of Sodom, Abraham courteously walking part of the way with them. When two of the men, to Abraham's view, were gone and only one remained, Abraham drew near to God. He had learned who his mysterious visitor was, and he had learned that judgment was about to fall on Sodom and Gomorrah because of their great wickedness. Some people might have said,

"That is what they deserve. They have had plenty of warnings and have not heeded them. Now let them perish." But that was not what Abraham thought and not what Abraham said; he was noble, magnanimous Abraham, the Friend of God.

Abraham drew near to God and began to plead for the wicked cities, asking if God would not spare them for the sake of the righteous men that lived there. Abraham did not know how few righteous men were there, but he began with fifty: "Peradventure there be fifty righteous within the city: wilt thou also destroy and not spare the place for the fifty righteous that are therein?. . . Shall not the judge of all the earth do right?" (Genesis 18:25-30).

Then God promised Abraham that He would spare the city if there were fifty righteous there. Then Abraham, with beautiful humility and yet angelic earnestness, said, "Behold now, I have taken upon me to speak unto the Lord, which am but dust and ashes. . . wilt Thou destroy all the city for the lack of five?" (verses 27-28).

And God said, "If I find there forty and five, I will not destroy it."

And so Abraham continued his pleading with God, asking that the place be spared for the sake of thirty righteous, and then for the sake of twenty, and finally for the sake of ten.

Alas, not even ten righteous could be found in Sodom. Destruction and death fell upon the city and all its inhabitants, save Lot and his daughters. But there is something deeply moving, infinitely tender and pathetic, wonderfully uplifting about that intercession of the friend of God for the wicked inhabitants of Sodom and Gomorrah. That is the way we ought to feel towards other people, and that is the way we ought to approach God and to pray to Him. Who knows how much you and I owe to those who have pled with God for our souls? Go, then, to the golden altar of prayer, and there offer your prayers in behalf of other souls.

> There is a place where thou canst touch the eyes
> Of blinded men to instant, perfect sight;

> There is a place where thou canst say, "Arise!"
> To dying captives, bound in chains of night;
> There is a place where thou canst reach the store
> Of hoarded gold and free it for the Lord;
> There is a place–upon some distant shore–
> Where thou canst send the worker or the Word;
> There is a place where Heaven's resistless power
> Responsive moves to thine insistent plea;
> There is a place–a silent, trusting hour–
> Where God Himself descends and fights for thee.
> Where is that blessed place–dost thou ask
> "Where?"
> O, Soul, it is the secret place of prayer.
> –Adelaide A. Pollard
> "The Indian Christian"

Jacob's Prayer

Another man whose prayer conquered God was Jacob. We have the record of that conquest in one of the most mysterious transactions of the Bible. There is something about it that appeals to us because of its very inscrutable mystery, and yet something there that appeals to us because we feel there is something in it that is deeply human. I refer to Jacob's midnight encounter with the angel on the fords of the Jabbok (Genesis 32:24-32).

It was twenty years since Jacob had deceived his dying father Isaac and cheated his brother Esau out of the blessing that belonged to the firstborn. During those two decades, although he had to struggle and fight for it, Jacob had found love, a home, and prosperity in Mesopotamia and now, a rich man, is returning to his father's country, when suddenly there falls across his path the shadow of his old transgression. He receives word that his brother Esau is on the march to meet him with four hundred armed men. Perhaps Jacob hoped that Esau was dead or, if living, that he had forgotten Jacob's great sin against him. Now he learns that Esau is on the march to meet him, Esau the cheated and the wronged, who had sworn an oath that he would kill his brother Jacob on sight.

Although distressed and frightened, Jacob's old cunning did not desert him. He divided his people and his flocks and herds into two bands and sent them on before him so that if Esau attacked one company, the other might escape. Then he made his prayer that God would deliver him out of the hand of Esau. He then sent messengers with costly presents to Esau, hoping thus to placate his brother. Having sent his company across the ford of the Jabbok, Jacob remained himself on the other side. "And Jacob was left alone!" This was to be the greatest experience of Jacob's life. It was an experience which came to him when he was left alone. Do not fear your solitary moments. God will come closer to you then than at any other time.

As Jacob stood there, alone in the shadows, "there wrestled a man with him until the breaking of the day." Who or what he was, Jacob did not know. But he did not seek to shun the battle or escape the encounter. All through the night the two antagonists fought there on the banks of the little stream. There was not a spectator to view their struggles. There was not a sound save the scuffling of their feet and the panting and labored breathing of the wrestlers. In awful solitude they fought. In the battle Jacob seemed to be getting the advantage so much so that his mysterious antagonist touched the hollow of his thigh and put it out of joint. Yet Jacob fought on, gripping his enemy all the more fiercely and tightly.

Then, as the morning dawned, Jacob suddenly learned that this midnight wrestler was not really an enemy but a friend, and as the angel hastened to be away with the dawning of the day, Jacob gripped him closely and cried, "I will not let thee go except thou bless me." Then the departing angel blessed Jacob and changed his name from Jacob, the supplanter, to Israel, prince with God, for, he said, "As a prince thou hast power with God and with men, and hast prevailed."

Application

In that night Jacob conquered God. Mysterious though that narrative is, rich are the treasures we find in it. What opposes us in life, what makes us struggle and plant and labor, is, after all, not an enemy but a friend in disguise. Do not mourn over the hard and difficult experiences of life, over the touches of providence that, as it were, have thrown your thigh out of joint, for in ways that you know not they have made you strong.

Still more is this true of our sorrows and our trials. At first they seem to come upon us with threat and anger, as that mysterious battler came upon Jacob there in the lonely watches of the night on the banks of the Jabbok. But their only purpose is to bless us, change us, to teach us how to pray, to transform our characters. Therefore, when these angels in disguise come upon you, hard though the battle is and desperate the encounter, heavy and labored though the breathing of the soul may be, make sure that you conquer God in them. Make sure that you utter the prayer of struggling Jacob, "I will not let thee go except thou bless me."

The Mother Who Conquered Christ

In the life of Christ Himself there is a beautiful and striking illustration of what He so frequently taught by parable and precept, the power of prayer to conquer God. In two of his parables, the Friend at Midnight (when the man knocked at the door of his unwilling neighbor until he came down and gave to him) and the parable of the Unjust Judge, who avenged the widow lest she weary him by her continual coming, Christ taught persistence and perseverance in prayer. But in His dealing with the Syro-Phoenician mother He Himself illustrated the power of earnest, effectual, God-conquering prayer (Mark 7:24-30).

Exposition

On the shores of Syria where Tyre once stood, you can still see the waves of the Mediterranean breaking over the prostrate pillars that once were the glory of Tyre. Standing there, one thinks of Tyre and its temples and its navies and of Nebuchadnezzar and Alexander who brought Tyre into the dust, but most of all of how a poor heart broken, gentile mother persuaded Jesus to heal her daughter.

This woman, probably a widow, had an only child, a daughter, who was grievously afflicted with an unclean spirit. When she heard that the great healer of Israel had come to their village, her heart beat high with hope. But when she spoke of the matter to her neighbors, they, no doubt, discouraged her. They probably said, "He will do nothing for you. Remember we are pagans and He is a Jew. Even if you get to where He is, His friends and disciples will not let you approach Him." But undeterred by their discouraging remarks, the woman made her appeal to Jesus, first of all, it would seem, on the street and then at the house. " Have mercy on me, O Lord, Thou Son of David. My daughter is grievously vexed with a devil." But what was the answer of Jesus? He answered her not a word! Nothing hurts, humiliates, and disconcerts, and sometimes angers like silence. I will make no attempt to explain the silence of Jesus, unless it was that He wanted not only to test out the faith and earnestness of this woman, but to encourage you and me in our prayers in those times when we pray and it seems that God is silent. His silence to Pilate, to Herod, and to those who mocked Him and cursed Him, we can understand, but how could He be silent to this heartbroken mother in her distress?

That silence would have frozen hope in the minds of most mothers, but not so this mother. She followed Jesus to the house where He was being entertained. There the irritated disciples said to Jesus, "Send her away for she crieth after us." Perhaps they meant "Lord, you might as well grant her request, for if you do not, she will keep on bothering us this way." Or it may have been just a suggestion that Jesus rid them of this nuisance. Then Jesus spoke for the first time, not to the woman but to the disciples, saying, "I am not sent but unto the lost sheep of the house of Israel. You know that my mission is to the Jews. It is not possible now for me to deal with those outside of Israel."

Then the poor woman, dropping the formal language in which she had first addressed Jesus as the Son of David, cried out, "Lord, Help me!" It was as if she had said, "Lord, I realize that I am not a Jew. I know that I have no claims upon Thee, but I am a poor broken-hearted mother. Lord, help me!" Then for the first time Jesus spoke to the woman herself. But what a speech it was! "Let the children first be filled, for it is not meet to take the children's bread and cast it unto the dogs." That evidently was a proverb, something like our, "Charity begins at home." It amounted to this, "Don't you know the proverb, woman, how it is not proper to take the children's bread and cast it to the dogs?" This, one would think, would have further humiliated and angered the woman. Had she not been likened to one of the dogs that prowl about the tables in that eastern land? But instead of being repulsed, this woman cried out the more earnestly and with a beautiful quickness and charm of speech, "Yes, Lord, I know that's so. But, Lord, even the dogs eat of the crumbs that fall from their master's table!" Then, Jesus, conquered by so wonderful a love and so invincible a faith, answered, "O woman, great is thy faith! Be it unto thee even as thou wilt!"

Application

There were two remarkable things about the great faith of this woman and her conquering prayer. The first thing was the *obstacles that her faith overcame*: the handicap of her pagan race, the discouragement of her neighbors, the rude discouragement of the disciples, the strange disconcerting silence of Jesus, and her seeming humiliation at His hands when He compared her to the outcast dogs. Every conceivable obstacle was there. But she overcame them all and today is immortal for her faith. The other remarkable thing about this *faith* is that *it was exercised, not for herself but for another.* Prayer reaches its grandest heights when we pray for another.

We all have difficulties in the way of our prayers and our faith. There are the discouragement of the world about us, the discouragement which comes from unworthy disciples of Christ, and the silence of God when we long to hear His voice. In these moments of discouragement and in the face of these difficulties, remember that mother who conquered Jesus by her prayers. For your own sake, and still more for the sake of others, keep on praying and hold on to your faith. Remember that you wield in your prayer the mightiest power, the power that moves the hand that moves the world.

God is a prayer-hearing and a prayer-answering God. He always answers. Let us be satisfied with His answers, whether or not they are the answers that we expected. Prayer is the key to the problems of our day; it locks the door that keeps out the doubts and dangers of the night. There are two prayers which we are encouraged to make, and about the answer to which there can be no doubt: one is, "Thy will be done"; the other, "God be merciful to me, a sinner." Christ heard that last prayer in His last hour on the Cross and was conquered by it, for He said to the penitent thief, "today shalt thou be with me in Paradise" (Luke 23:43).

The Prayers of the Bible

Dwight Lyman Moody (1837-1899) is known
around the world as one of America's most
effective evangelists. Converted as a teenager
through the witness of his Sunday School teacher,
Moody became active in YMCA and Sunday
School work in Chicago while pursuing a
successful business career. He then devoted his
full time to evangelism and was mightily used of
God in campaigns in both the United States and
Great Britain. He founded the Northfield School
for Girls, the Mount Hermon School for Boys, the
Northfield Bible Conference, and the Moody Bible
Institute in Chicago. Before the days of planes
and radio, Moody traveled more than a million
miles and addressed more than 100 million
people. This message on prayer is from *The Best of
D.L. Moody*, edited by Ralph Turnbull and
published by Baker Book House.

2

THE PRAYERS OF THE BIBLE

THOSE WHO have left the deepest impression on this sin-cursed earth have been men and women of prayer. You will find that prayer has been the mighty power that has moved not only God, but man. Abraham was a man of prayer, and angels came down from heaven to converse with him. Jacob's prayer was answered in the wonderful interview at Peniel, that resulted in his having such a mighty blessing, and in the softening of the heart of his brother Esau; the child Samuel was given in answer to Hannah's prayer; Elijah's prayer closed up the heavens for three years and six months, and he prayed again and the heavens gave rain.

Bible Men Who Prayed

The Apostle James tells us that the prophet Elijah was a man "subject to like passions as we are." I am thankful that those men and women who were so mighty in prayer were just like us. We are apt to think that those prophets and mighty men and women of old time were different from what we are. To be sure they lived in a much darker age, but they were of like passions with ourselves.

We read that on another occasion Elijah brought down fire on Mount Carmel. The prophets of Baal had cried long and loud, but no answer came. The God of Elijah heard and answered his prayer. Let us remember that the God of Elijah still lives. The prophet was translated and went up to heaven, but his God still lives, and we have the same access to Him that Elijah had. We have the same warrant to go to God and ask the fire from heaven to come down and consume our lusts and passions, to burn up our dross, and to let Christ shine through us.

Elisha prayed, and life came back to a dead child. Many of our children are dead in trespasses and sins. Let us do as Elisha did; let us entreat God to raise them up in answer to our prayers. Manasseh, the king, was a wicked man and had done everything he could against the God of his father; yet in Babylon, when he cried to God, his cry was heard, and he was taken out of prison and put on the throne at Jerusalem. Surely if God gave heed to the prayer of wicked Manasseh, He will hear ours in the time of our distress. Is not this a time of distress with a great number of people? Let us pray and remember that *God answers prayer.*

Look, again, at Samson. He prayed, and his strength came back, so that he slew more at his death than during his life. He was a restored backslider, and he had power with God. If those who are backsliders will return to God, they will see how quickly God will answer prayer.

Job prayed, and his captivity was turned. Light came in the place of darkness, and God lifted him up above the height of his former prosperity in answer to prayer.

Daniel prayed to God, and Gabriel came to tell him that he was a man greatly beloved of God. Three times that message came to him from heaven in answer to prayer. The secrets of heaven were imparted to him, and he was told that God's Son was going to be cut off for the sins of His people.

We find also that Cornelius prayed, and Peter was sent to tell him words whereby he and his should be saved. In answer to prayer this great blessing came upon him and his household. Peter had gone up to the house top to pray in the afternoon, when he had that wonderful vision of the sheet let down from heaven. It was when prayer was made without ceasing unto God for Peter that the angel was sent to deliver him.

So all through the Scriptures you will find that when believing prayer went up to God, the answer came down. I think it would be a very interesting study to go right through the Bible and see what has happened while God's people have been on their knees calling upon Him. Certainly the study would greatly strengthen our faith by showing, as it would, how wonderfully God has heard and delivered when the cry has gone up to Him for help.

Look at Paul and Silas in the prison at Philippi. As they prayed and sang praises, the place was shaken, and the jailer was converted. Probably that one conversion has done more than any other recorded in the Bible to bring people into the kingdom of God. How many have been blessed in seeking to answer the question, "What must I do to be saved?" It was the prayer of those two godly men that brought the jailer to his knees and that brought blessing to him and his family.

You remember how Stephen, as he prayed and looked up, saw the heavens opened and the Son of Man at the right hand of God; the light of heaven fell on his face so that it shone. Remember, too, how the face of Moses shone as he came down from the Mount; he had been in communion with God, He lifts His countenance upon us, and instead of our having gloomy looks, our faces will shine because God has heard and answered our prayers.

Christ Prayed

We read that the Lord Jesus Christ prayed to His Father for everything. Every great crisis in His life was preceded by prayer. Notice that Christ was praying at His baptism. As He prayed, the heaven was opened, and the Holy Ghost descended on Him.

Another great event in His life was His Transfiguration. "As He prayed, the fashion of His countenance was altered, and His raiment was white and glistening" (Luke 9:29).

We read again: "It came to pass in those days, that He went out into a mountain to pray, and continued all night in prayer to God" (Luke 6:12). This is the only place where it is recorded that the Savior spent a whole night in prayer. What was about to take place? When He came down from the mountain, He gathered His disciples around Him and preached that great discourse known as the Sermon on the Mount, the most wonderful sermon that has ever been preached to mortal men. Probably no sermon has done so much good, and it was preceded by a night of prayer. Prayer precedes power.

In John 11:41-42, we read that Jesus at the grave of Lazarus lifted up His eyes to heaven and said: "Father, I thank thee that thou hast heard me; and I know that thou hearest me always: but because of the people which stand by I said it, that they may believe that thou hast sent Me." Notice that before He spoke the dead to life, He spoke to His Father. If our spiritually dead ones are to be raised, we must have power with God. Jesus was in communion with His Father, and so He could be assured that His prayers were heard.

We read again, in John 12:27, that He prayed to the Father. I think this is one of the saddest chapters in the whole Bible. He was about to leave the Jewish nation and to make atonement for the sin of the world. Hear what He says: "Now is my soul troubled; and what shall I say? Father, save Me from this hour; but for this cause came I unto this hour." He was almost under the shadow of the Cross; the iniquities of mankind were about to be laid upon Him; one of His twelve disciples was going to deny Him and swear he never knew Him; another was to sell Him for thirty pieces of silver; all were to forsake Him and flee. His soul was exceedingly sorrowful, and He prays; when His soul was troubled, God spoke to Him. Then in the Garden of Gethsemane, while He prayed, an angel appeared to strengthen Him. In answer to His cry, "Father, glorify Thy Name," He hears a voice "I have both glorified it, and will glorify it again" (John 12:28).

Another memorable prayer of our Lord was in the Garden of Gethsemane: "He was withdrawn from them about a stone's cast, and kneeled down, and prayed (Luke 23:41). I would draw your attention to the recorded fact that four times the answer came right down from heaven while the Savior prayed to God. The first time was at His baptism when the heavens were opened and the Spirit descended upon Him in answer to His prayer. Again, on the Mount of Transfiguration, God appeared and spoke to Him. Then when the Greeks desired to see Him, the voice of God was heard responding to His call; and again, when He cried to the Father in the midst of His agony, a direct response was given. These things are recorded, I doubt not, that we may be encouraged to pray.

We read that His disciples came to Him and said, "Lord, teach us to pray." It is not recorded that He taught them how to preach. I have often said that I would rather know how to pray like Daniel than to preach like Gabriel. If you get love into your soul so that the grace of God may come down in answer to prayer, there will be no trouble about reaching the people. It is not by eloquent sermons that perishing souls are going to be reached; we need the power of God to meet their needs.

The prayer our Lord taught His disciples is commonly called the Lord's Prayer. I think that the Lord's prayer, more properly, is that in John chapter 17. That is the longest prayer on record that Jesus made. You can read it slowly and carefully in about four or five minutes. I think we may learn a lesson here. Our Master's prayers were short when offered in public; when He was alone with God, He could spend the whole night in communion with His Father. My experience is that those who pray most in their closets generally make short prayers in public. Long prayers are too often not prayers at all, and they weary the people. How short the publican's prayer was: "God be merciful to me a sinner" (Luke 18:13). The prayer of the thief on the cross was a short one: "Lord, remember me when Thou comest into Thy Kingdom!" (Luke 23:42). Peter's prayer was, "Lord save me" (Matthew 14:30). So, if you go through the Scriptures, you will find that the prayers that brought immediate answers were generally brief. Let our prayers be to the point, just telling God what we want.

In the prayer of our Lord, in John 17, we find that He made seven requests: one for Himself, four for His disciples around Him, and two for the disciples of succeeding ages. Six times in that one prayer He repeats that God had sent Him. The world looked upon Him as an imposter; He wanted them to know that He was heaven-sent. He speaks of the world nine times, and mentions His disciples and those who believe on Him fifty times.

Christ's last prayer on the cross was a short one. "Father, forgive them; for they know not what they do" (Luke

23:34). I believe that prayer was answered. We find that right there in front of the cross, a Roman centurion was converted. It was probably in answer to the Savior's prayer. The conversion of the thief, I believe, was in answer to that prayer of our blessed Lord. Saul of Tarsus may have heard it, and the words may have followed him as he traveled to Damascus so that when the Lord spoke to him on the way, he may have recognized the voice. One thing we do know, that on the day of Pentecost some of the enemies of the Lord were converted. Surely that was in answer to the prayer, "Father, forgive them!"

Hence, we see that prayer holds a high place among the exercises of a spiritual life. All God's people have been praying people. Martin Luther and his companions were men of such mighty pleading with God that they broke the spell of ages and laid nations subdued at the foot of the Cross. When John Knox grasped all Scotland in his strong arms of faith, his prayers terrified tyrants. George Whitefield, after much holy, faithful close-pleading, went to the Devil's fair and in one day took more than a thousand souls out of the paw of the lion. See a praying Wesley turn more than ten thousand souls to the Lord! Look at the praying Charles Finney, whose prayers, faith, sermons, and writings shook this country and sent a wave of blessing through two continents.

Dr. Thomas Guthrie speaks of the need of:

> The first true sign of spiritual life, prayer, is also the means of maintaining it. Man can as well live physically without breathing, as spiritually without praying. There is a class of animals—the cetaceous, neither fish nor sea-fowl—that inhabit the deep. It is their home, they never leave it for the shore; yet, though swimming beneath its waves, and sounding its darkest depths, they have ever and anon to rise to the surface that they may breathe the air. Without that, these monarchs of the deep could not exist. And something like what is imposed on them by a physical necessity, the Christian has to do by a spiritual one. It is by ever and anon ascending up to God, by rising through prayer into a loftier, purer region for supplies of divine grace, that he maintains his spiritual life. Prevent

these animals from rising to the surface, and they die for want of breath; prevent the Christian from rising to God, and he dies for want of prayer.

"Since I began," said Dr. Payson when a student, "to beg God's blessing on my studies, I have done more in one week than in the whole year before." Luther, when most pressed with work, said, "I have so much to do that I cannot get on without three hours a day praying." And not only do theologians think and speak highly of prayer; men of all ranks and positions in life have felt the same. General Havelock rose at four o'clock, if the hour for marching was six rather than lose the precious privilege of communion with God before setting out. Sir Matthew Hale says: "If I omit praying and reading God's Word in the morning, nothing goes well all day."

"A great part of my time," said Robert McCheyne, "is spent in getting my heart in tune for prayer. It is the link that connects earth with heaven."

Essential Elements to Prayer

There are nine elements which are essential of true prayer. The first is *adoration*; we cannot meet God on a level at the start. We must approach Him as One far beyond our reach or sight. The next is *confession*; sin must be put out of the way. We cannot have any real communion with God while there is any transgression between us. *Restitution* is another; we have to make good the wrong, wherever possible. *Thanksgiving* is the next; we must be thankful for what God has done for us already. Then comes *forgiveness*,and then *unity*; and then for prayer, such as these things produce, there must be *faith*. Thus influenced, we shall be ready to offer direct *petition*. We hear a good deal of praying that is just exhorting, and if you did not see the man's eyes closed, you would suppose he was preaching. Then, much that is called prayer is simply finding fault. There needs to be more *petition* in our prayers. After all these, there must come *submission*. While praying, we must be ready to accept the will of God.

The Throne of Grace

Charles Haddon Spurgeon (1834-1892) is
undoubtedly the most famous minister of modern
times. Converted in 1850, he united with the
Baptists and very soon began to preach in various
places. He became pastor of the Baptist church in
Waterbeach in 1851, and three years later he was
called to the decaying Park Street Church,
London. Within a short time, the work began to
prosper, a new church was built and dedicated in
1861, and Spurgeon became London's most
popular preacher. In 1855, he began to publish his
sermons weekly, and today they make up the
forty-nine volumes of *The Metropolitan
Tabernacle Pulpit.* He founded a pastors' college
and several orphanages. This sermon is taken
from *The Metropolitan Tabernacle Pulpit.*

C.H. Spurgeon

3

THE THRONE OF GRACE

The throne of grace (Hebrews 4:16).

THESE WORDS are found embedded in that gracious verse, "Let us therefore come boldly unto the throne of grace, that we may obtain mercy, and find grace to help in time of need" and are a gem in a golden setting. True prayer is an approach of the soul by the Spirit of God to the throne of God. It is not the utterance of words, nor is it alone the feeling of desires, but it is the advance of the desires to God, the spiritual approach of our nature towards the Lord our God. True prayer is not a mere mental exercise, nor a vocal performance, but it is deeper far than that – it is spiritual communion with the Creator of heaven and earth. God is a Spirit unseen of mortal eye and only to be perceived by the inner man; our spirit within us, begotten by the Holy Ghost at our regeneration. Prayer is a spiritual business from beginning to end, and its aim and object end not with man, but reach to God Himself.

True Prayer

For such prayer the work of the Holy Ghost Himself is needed. If prayer were of the lips alone, we should only need breath in our nostrils to pray. If prayer were of the desires alone, many excellent desires are easily felt, even by natural men. But when it is the spiritual desire, and the spiritual fellowship of the human spirit with the Great Spirit, then the Holy Ghost Himself must be present all through it to help infirmity and give life and power, or else true prayer will never be presented. The thing offered to God will wear the name and have the form, but the inner life of prayer will be far from it.

Moreover, it is clear from the connection of our text that the interposition of the Lord Jesus Christ is essential to acceptable prayer. As prayer will not be truly prayer without the Spirit of God, so it will not be prevailing prayer without the Son of God. He, the Great High Priest, must go within the veil for us; through His crucified person the veil must be entirely taken away. Until then, we are shut out from the living God. The man who, despite the teaching of Scripture, tries to pray without a Savior insults the Deity, and he who imagines that his own natural desires, coming up before God unsprinkled with the precious blood, will be an acceptable sacrifice before God, makes a mistake. He has not brought an offering that God can accept.

Approaching the Divine King

Our text speaks of *throne* – "The Throne of Grace." God is to be viewed in prayer as our Father; that is the aspect which is dearest to us. But still we are not to regard Him as though He were such as we are; for our Savior has qualified the expression "Our Father" with the words "who art in heaven." And close at the heels of that condescending name, in order to remind us that our Father is still infinitely greater than we, He has bidden us say, "Hallowed be thy name; thy kingdom come," so that our Father is still to be regarded as a King. Therefore, in prayer we come, not only to our Father's feet, but we come also to the throne of the Great Monarch of the universe. The mercyseat is a throne, and we must not forget this.

The Need for Humble Worship

If prayer should always be regarded by us as an entrance into the courts of the royalty of heaven and if we are to behave ourselves as courtiers should act in the presence of an illustrious majesty, then we are not at a loss to know the right spirit in which to pray. If in prayer we come to a throne, it is clear that our spirit should, in the first place, be one of lowly reverence. It is expected that the subject in approaching to the king should pay him homage and honor. In our case, the king before whom we come is the highest of all monarchs, the King of kings, the Lord of lords. Emperors are but the shadows of

His imperial power. They call themselves kings by right divine, but what divine right have they? Common sense laughs their pretensions to scorn. The Lord alone hath divine right, and to Him only does the kingdom belong. He is the blessed and only potentate.

Besides, He is the most holy of all kings. His throne is a great white throne, unspotted and clear as crystal. "The heavens are not pure in his sight, and he charged his angels with folly" (Job 4:18). And you, a sinful creature, with what lowliness should you draw near to Him? Familiarity there may be, but let it not be unhallowed. *Boldness there should be, but let it not be impertinent.* Still you are on earth and He in heaven; still you are a worm of the dust, a creature crushed before the moth, and He the Everlasting. Before the mountains were brought forth He was God, and if all created things should pass away again, yet still were He the same. I am afraid we do not bow as we should before the Eternal Majesty; but, henceforth, let us ask the Spirit of God to put us in a right frame of mind so that every one of our prayers may be a reverential approach to the Infinite Majesty above.

The Need for Joyful Prayer

His throne, therefore, in the second place, is to be approached with devout joyfulness. If I find myself favored by divine grace to stand among those favored ones who frequent His courts, shall I not feel glad? I might have been in His prison, but I am before His throne; I might have been driven from His presence for ever, but I am permitted to come near to Him, even into His royal palace, into His secret chamber of gracious audience; shall I not then be thankful? Shall not my thankfulness ascend into joy, and shall I not feel that I am honored and that I am made the recipient of great favors when I am permitted to pray?

Why is your countenance sad, O suppliant, when you stand before the throne of grace? Christian, since you are now favored to come before the King in His silken robes of love, let your face shine with sacred delight. If your sorrows are heavy, tell them unto Him, for He can assuage them; if your sins are multiplied, confess them, for He can forgive them. O courtiers in the halls of such a Monarch, be exceedingly glad and mingle praises with your prayers.

The Need for Prayerful Submission

It is a throne, and therefore, in the third place, whenever it is approached, it should be with complete submission. We do not pray to God to instruct Him as to what He ought to do; neither for a moment must we presume to dictate the line of the divine procedure. We are permitted to say to God, "Thus and thus would we have it," but we must always add, "but, seeing that we are ignorant and may be mistaken—seeing that we are still in the flesh, and, therefore, may be actuated by carnal motives—not as we will but as Thou wilt." Who shall dictate to the throne? No loyal child of God will for a moment imagine that he is to occupy the place of the King, but he bows before Him who has a right to be Lord of all.

Therefore, though he utters his desire earnestly, vehemently, and very urgently, and pleads and pleads again, yet it is always with this needful reservation: "Thy will be done, my Lord, and, if I ask anything that is not in accordance with Thy will, my inmost will is that Thou wouldst be good enough to deny thy servant; I will take it as a true answer if Thou refuse me, if I ask that which seemeth not good in Thy sight." Therefore will I speak with the deepest submission to Thy divine decrees."

The Need for Enlarged Expectations

But, in the fourth place, if it be a throne, it ought to be approached with enlarged expectations. Well does our hymn put it:

Thou art coming to a king, large petitions with thee bring.

We do not come, as it were, in prayer only to God's benevolence fund where He dispenses His favors to the poor, nor do we come to the back door of the house of mercy to receive the broken scraps, though that is more than we deserve; to eat the crumbs that fall from the Master's table is more than we could claim. But when we pray, we are standing in the palace, on the glittering floor of the great King's own reception room, and thus we are placed upon a vantage ground. In prayer we stand where angels bow with veiled faces; there, even there, the cherubim and seraphim adore, before that same throne to which our prayers ascend. And shall we come there with stunted requests and narrow and contracted faith? No, it does not become a king to be giving away pennies and nickels; he distributes large pieces of gold.

Beware of imagining that God's thoughts are as your thoughts and that His ways as your ways. Do not bring before God stinted petitions and narrow desires by saying, "Lord, do according to these," but, remember, as high as the heavens are above the earth, so high are His ways above your ways and His thoughts above your thoughts. Ask, therefore, in a God-like way for great things, for you are before a great throne. Oh, that we always felt this way when we came before the throne of grace, for then He would do for us exceeding abundantly above what we ask or even think.

The Need for Full Confidence

And, beloved, I may add, in the fifth place, that the right spirit in which to approach the throne of grace is that of unstaggering confidence. Who shall doubt the King? Who dares impugn the Imperial word? It was well said that if integrity were banished from the hearts of all mankind besides, it ought still to dwell in the hearts of kings. Shame on a king if he can lie. The lowliest beggar in the streets is dishonored by a broken promise, but what shall we say of a king if his word cannot be depended upon? Oh, shame upon us if we are unbelieving before the throne of the King of heaven and earth. With our God before us in all His glory sitting on the throne of grace, will our hearts dare to say we mistrust Him? Such blasphemous thoughts should be banished, and if they

must come, let them come upon us when we are somewhere in the outskirts of His dominions, if such a place
there be, but not in prayer when we are in His immediate
presence and behold Him in all the glory of His throne of
grace. There, surely is the place for the child to trust its
Father, for the loyal subject to trust his monarch; therefore, far from it should be all wavering or suspicion.
Unstaggering faith should be predominant before the
mercyseat.

The Need for Genuiness in Prayer

We offer only one other remark upon this point, that if
prayer is a coming before the throne of God, it ought
always to be conducted with deepest sincerity, and in the
spirit which makes everything *real*. If you are disloyal
enough to despise the King, at least, for your own sake,
do not mock Him to His face and when He is upon His
throne. If anywhere you dare repeat holy words without
heart, let it not be in Jehovah's palace. If a person should
ask for audience with royalty and then should say, "I
hardly know why I have come, I do not know that I have
anything very particular to ask; I have no very urgent
request," would he not be guilty both of folly and base-
ness?

As for our great King, when we venture into His presence, let us have an errand there. Let us beware of playing at praying. It is insolence towards God. If I am called
upon to pray in public, I must not dare to use words that
are intended to please the ears of my fellow-worshippers,
but I must realize that I am speaking to God Himself and
that I have business to transact with the great Lord. And
in my private prayer, if when I rise from my bed in the
morning, I bow my knee and repeat certain words, or
when I retire to rest at night and go through the same
regular form, I rather sin than do anything that is good
unless my very soul speaks unto the Most High.

Do you think that the King of heaven is delighted to
hear you pronounce words with a frivolous tongue and a
thoughtless mind? You do not know Him. He is a Spirit,

and they that worship Him must worship Him in spirit and in truth. From all the spirits that behold the face of our Father who is in heaven, even now, I hear a voice which says, "Oh come, let us worship and bow down; let us kneel before the Lord our maker. For he is our God; and we are the people of his pasture, and the sheep of his hand" (Psalm 95:6-7). "O worship the Lord in the beauty of holiness: fear before him, all the earth" (Psalm 96:9).

Prayer in the Presence of God's Grace

So that the glow and brilliance of the word *throne* should not be too much for mortal vision, our text now presents us with the soft, gentle radiance of that delightful word–*grace*. We are called to the throne of *grace*, not to the throne of law. Rocky Sinai once was the throne of law when God came to Paran with ten thousand of His holy ones. Who desired to draw near to that throne? Even Israel might not. Bounds were set about the mount, and if but a beast touched the mount, it was stoned or thrust through with a sword. O you self-righteous ones who hope that you can obey the law and think that you can be saved by it, look to the flames that Moses saw and shrink and tremble and despair. To that throne we do not come now, for through Jesus the case is changed.

And, blessed be God, we are not now speaking of the throne of ultimate justice. Before that we shall come, and as many of us as have believed will find it to be a throne of grace as well as of justice; for He who sits upon that throne shall pronounce no sentence of condemnation against the man who is justified by faith.

But I do not have to call you now to the place from which the resurrection-trumpet shall ring out so shrill and clear. We are still on praying ground and pleading terms with God, and the throne to which we are bidden to come, and of which we speak at this time, is the throne of grace. It is a throne set up on purpose for *the dispensation of grace,* a throne from which every utterance *is an utterance of grace*; the scepter that is stretched out from it is the silver *scepter of grace*; the decrees proclaimed from it are *purposes of grace*; the gifts that are scattered down its golden steps are *gifts of grace*; and He that sits upon the throne is grace itself. It is the throne of grace to which we approach when we pray, and let us for a moment or two think this over, by way of consolatory encouragement to those who are beginning to pray; indeed, this truth comes to all of us who are praying men and women.

Grace for Imperfect Prayers

If in prayer I come before a throne of grace, then the faults of my prayer will be overlooked. In beginning to pray, dear friends, you feel as if you did not pray. The groanings of your spirit when you rise from your knees are such that you think there is nothing in them. What a blotted, blurred, smeared prayer is it. Never mind; you have not come to the throne of justice. Otherwise, when God perceived the fault in the prayer He would spurn it – your broken words, your gaspings, and your stammerings are before a throne of grace.

Our condescending King does not maintain a stately etiquette in his court like that which has been observed by princes among men, where a little mistake or a flaw would secure the petitioner's being dismissed with disgrace. Oh, no, the faulty cries of His children are not severely criticized by Him. The Lord High Chamberlain of the palace above, our Lord Jesus Christ, takes care to alter and amend every prayer before He presents it, and He makes the prayer perfect with His perfection and prevalent with His own merits. God looks upon the prayer as presented through Christ and forgives all its own inherent faultiness.

How this ought to encourage any of us who feel ourselves to be feeble, wandering, and unskillful in prayer. If you cannot plead with God as sometimes you did in years gone by, if you feel as if somehow or other you had grown rusty in the work of supplication, never give up, but come still, yes and come oftener, for it is not a throne of severe criticism, but to a throne of grace you come.

Grace for Praying Sinners

Then, further, inasmuch as it is a throne of grace, the faults of the petitioner himself shall not prevent the success of his prayer. Oh, what faults there are in us! To come before a throne how unfit we are—we that are all defiled with sin within and without! Do any of you dare think of praying if it were not that God's throne is a throne of grace? If you could, I confess I could not. An absolute God, infinitely holy and just, could not in consistency with His divine nature answer any prayer from such a sinner as I am if it were not that He has arranged a plan by which my prayer comes up no longer to a throne of absolute justice, but to a throne which is also the mercyseat, the propitiation, the place where God meets sinners through Jesus Christ. Ah, I could not say to you, "Pray," not even to you saints, unless it were a throne of grace, much less could I talk of prayer to you sinners.

But now I will say this to every sinner here, though he should think himself to be the worst sinner that ever lived, cry unto the Lord and seek Him while He may be found. A throne of grace is a place fitted for you to go to your knees and by simple faith go to your Savior, for He it is who is the throne of grace. It is in Him that God is able to dispense grace unto the most guilty of mankind. Blessed be God, neither the faults of the prayer nor yet of the suppliant shall shut out our petitions from God who delights in broken and contrite hearts.

God's Gracious Help in Prayer

If it is a throne of grace, then the desires of the pleader will be interpreted. If I cannot find words in which to utter my desires, God in His grace will read my desires without the words. He takes the meaning of His saints, the meaning of their groans. A throne that was not gracious would not trouble itself to make out our petitions, but God, the infinitely gracious one, will dive into the soul of our desires and will read there what we cannot speak with the tongue. Have you never seen a parent when his child is trying to say something to him, and he knows very well what it is the little one has got to say, help him over the words and utter the syllables for him? If the little one has half-forgotten what he would say, you have heard the father suggest the word.

Similarly, the ever-blessed Spirit, from the throne of grace, will help us and teach us words and even write in our hearts the desires themselves. The Spirit will direct your desires to the things for which you ought to seek; He will teach you your wants, though as yet you know them not; He will suggest to you His promises that you may be able to plead them; He will, in fact, be Alpha and Omega to your prayer, just as He is to your salvation.

For as salvation is from first to last of grace, so the sinner's approach to the throne of grace is of grace from first to last. What comfort this is. Will we not, my dear friends, with the greater boldness draw near to this throne, as we learn the sweet meaning of His precious words, "the throne of grace"?

God's Provision by Grace

If it be a throne of grace, then all the needs of those who come to it will be supplied. The King from such a throne will not say, "Thou must bring to me gifts, thou must offer to me sacrifices." It is not a throne for receiving tribute; it is a throne for dispensing gifts. Come, then, you who are poor as poverty itself; come you that have no merits and are destitute of virtues; come you that are reduced to a beggarly bankruptcy by Adam's fall and by your own transgressions. This is not the throne of majesty which supports itself by the taxation of its subjects, but a throne which glorifies itself by streaming forth like a fountain with floods of good things. Come now, and receive the wine and milk which are freely given; yes, come buy wine and milk without money and without price. All the petitioner's needs will be supplied because it is a throne of grace.

God's Compassion for Those Who Pray

And as a result, God will show compassion for all the petitioner's miseries. Suppose I come to the throne of grace with the burden of my sins; there is one on the throne who felt the burden of sin in ages long gone by and has not forgotten its weight. Suppose I come loaded with sorrow; there is one who knows all the sorrows to which humanity can be subjected. Am I depressed and distressed? Do I fear that God himself has forsaken me? There is one upon the throne who said, "My God, my God, why hast thou forsaken me?" It is a throne from which grace delights to look upon the miseries of mankind with tender eye to consider them and to relieve them.

"The throne of grace." The phrase grows as I turn it over in my mind, and to me it is a most delightful reflection that if I come to the throne of God in prayer, I may feel a thousand defects, but yet there is hope. I usually feel more dissatisfied with my prayers than with anything else I do. I do not believe that it is an easy thing to pray in public so as to conduct the devotions of a large congregation aright. We sometimes hear persons commended for preaching well, but if any shall be enabled to pray well, there will be an equal gift and a higher grace in it. But suppose in our prayers there should be defects of knowledge; it is a throne of grace, and our Father knows defects of faith; He sees our little faith and still does not reject it, small as it is. He does not in every case measure out His gifts by the degree of our faith, but by the sincerity and trueness of faith.

And if there should be grave defects in our spirit and failures in the fervency or in the humility of the prayer, though these should not be there and are much to be deplored, grace overlooks and forgives all this, and still its merciful hand is stretched out to enrich us according to our needs. Surely this ought to induce many to pray who have not prayed and should make us who have been long accustomed to use the consecrated art of prayer to draw near with greater boldness than ever to the throne.

God's Grace on the Throne

But, now regarding our text as a whole, it conveys to us the idea of grace enthroned. It is a throne, and who sits on it? It is grace personified that is here installed in dignity. And, truly, today grace is on a throne. In the gospel of Jesus Christ grace is the most predominant attribute of God. How comes it to be so exalted? We reply that grace has a throne by *conquest*. Grace came down to earth in the form of the Well-beloved, and it met with sin. Long and sharp was the struggle, and grace appeared to be trampled under foot of sin. But grace at last seized sin, threw it on its own shoulders; and, though all but crushed beneath the burden, grace carried sin up to the cross and nailed it there, slew it there, put it to death for ever, and triumphed gloriously.

Grace, moreover, sits on the throne because it has established itself by *right*. There is no injustice in the grace of God. God is as just when He forgives a believer as when He casts a sinner into hell. I believe in my own soul that there is as much and as pure a justice in the acceptance of a soul that believes in Christ as there will be in the rejection of those souls who die impenitent and are banished from Jehovah's presence. The sacrifice of Christ has enabled God to be just, and yet the justifier of him that believeth. He who knows the word *substitution* and can understand its meaning aright will see that there is nothing due to punitive justice from any believer since Jesus Christ has paid all the believer's debts.

Grace is enthroned this day because Christ has finished His work and gone into the heavens. It is enthroned in *power*.

Sinner, saint, oh, when grace sits on the throne, I beseech you close in with it at once. It can be no higher, it can be no greater, for it is written "God is love," which is an alias for grace. Oh, come and bow before it; come and adore the infinite mercy and grace of God.

I say, then, that grace is enthroned by conquest, by right, and by power, and, I will add, it is enthroned in *glory*, for God glorifies His grace. It is one of His objects now to make His grace illustrious. He delights to pardon penitents and so to show His pardoning grace; He delights to look upon wanderers and restore them, to show His reclaiming grace; He delights to look upon the broken-hearted and comfort them so that He may show His consoling grace. Believe this, you can come at once and glorify grace by becoming instances of its power.

God's Gracious Covenant and Our Prayers

On the throne of grace, sovereignty has placed itself under bonds of love. God will do as He wills; but on the mercyseat He is under bonds – bonds of His own making – for He has entered into covenant with Christ, and thus into covenant with His chosen. Though God is and ever must be a sovereign, He never will break His covenant nor alter the word that is gone out of His mouth. He cannot be false to a covenant of His own making.

Moreover, on the throne of grace, God is again bound to us by His promises. The covenant contains in it many gracious promises, exceedingly great and precious. "Ask and it shall be given you; seek, and ye shall find; knock, and it shall be opened unto you" (Matthew 7:7). Until God had said that word or a word to that effect, it was at His own option to hear prayer or not, but it is not so now; for now, if it is true prayer offered through Jesus Christ, His truth binds Him to hear it.

And it is the sweetest thought of all that every covenant promise has been endorsed and sealed with blood, and far be it from the everlasting God to pour scorn upon the blood of His dear Son. When a king has given a charter to a city, he may have previously been absolute, and there may have been nothing to check his prerogatives, but when the city has its charter, then it pleads its rights before the king.

It is not possible that we can plead in vain with God when we plead the blood-sealed covenant, ordered in all things and sure. Heaven and earth shall pass away but the power of the blood of Jesus with God can never fail. It speaks when we are silent, and it prevails when we are defeated. Christian, let us come boldly, for we bear the promise in our hearts. May God the Holy Spirit help us to use aright from this time forward "the throne of grace."

Prayer

Frederick W. Robertson (1816-1853) wanted to be a soldier, but he yielded to his father's decision that he take orders in the Anglican church. The courage that he would have shown on the battlefields, he displayed in the pulpit, where he fearlessly declared truth as he saw it. Never strong physically, he experienced deep depression, he questioned his faith, and he often wondered if his ministry was doing any good. He died a young man, in great pain, but in faith and courage. He had ministered for only six years at Trinity Chapel, Brighton, but today his printed sermons have taken his brave message around the world. This one is from his *Sermons, Fourth Series*, published in 1900 in London by Kegan Paul, Trench, Trubner, and Company.

Frederick W. Robertson

4

PRAYER

And he went a little farther, and fell on his face, and prayed, saying, O my father, if it be possible, let this cup pass from me: nevertheless not as I will, but as thou *wilt* (Matthew 26:39).

NO ONE WILL refuse to identify holiness with prayer. To say that a man is religious, is the same thing as to say he prays. For what is prayer? It is to connect every thought with the thought of God, to look on everything as His work and His appointment, to submit every thought, wish, and resolve to Him to feel His presence so that it shall restrain us even in our wildest joy. That is prayer. And what we are now, surely we are by prayer. If we have attained any measure of goodness, if we have resisted temptations, if we have any self-command, or if we live with aspirations and desires beyond the common, we shall not hesitate to ascribe all to prayer.

There is, therefore, no question among Christians about the efficacy of prayer; but even when that is granted generally, then questionings and diversities of view begin. What is prayer? What is the efficacy of prayer? Is prayer necessarily words in form and sequence; or is there a real prayer that can never be verbalized? Does prayer change the outward universe, or does it alter our inward being? Does it work on God, or does it work on us?

To all these questions, I believe a full and sufficient answer is returned in the text. Let us examine it calmly, and without prejudice or prepossession. If we do, we shall obtain a conclusion in which we may rest with peace, no matter what we conclude. We will consider: 1) The right of petition, 2) erroneous views of prayer, and 3) the true efficacy of prayer.

The Right of Petition

"Let this cup pass from me." We infer prayer to be a *right* because it is a necessity of our human nature.

The Son of Man feels the hour at hand: shrinks from it, seeks solitude, flees from human society, feels the need of it again, and goes back to His disciples. Here is that need of sympathy which forces us to desire congenial thought among others, and here is that recoil from cold unsympathizing people which forces us back to our loneliness again. In such an hour, they who have before forgotten prayer flee to God, and in such an hour, even the most resigned are not without the wish, "Let this cup pass." Christ Himself has a separate wish–one human wish.

Prayer, then, is a necessity of our humanity rather than a duty. To force it as a duty is dangerous. Christ did not; He never commanded it and never taught it until asked. This necessity is twofold. First, there is the necessity of sympathy. We touch other human spirits only at a point or two. In the deepest departments of thought and feeling, we are alone, and the desire to escape that loneliness finds for itself a voice in prayer.

Next, there is the necessity of escaping the sense of a crushing fate. The feeling that all things are fixed and unalterable, that we are surrounded by necessities which we cannot break through, is intolerable whenever it is realized. Our egotism cries against it–our innocent egotism. As a result the practical reconciliation between our innocent egotism and hideous fatalism is prayer, which realizes a living Person ruling all things with a will.

Again, we base this right on our privilege as children. "My father"–the sonship that Christ shares with us reveals the human race as a family in which God is a Father and He is the elder brother. It would be a strange family where the child's will dictates; but it would also be strange where a child may not, as a child, express its foolish wish, even if it is only to have the impossibility of gratifying it explained.

Christ used it as a right, therefore we may. There are many cases in life where to act seems useless and many truths which at times appear incredible. Then we throw ourselves on Him – He did it, He believed it, that is enough. He was wise where I am foolish. He was holy where I am evil. He must know. He must be right. I rely on Him.

Bring what arguments you may. Say that prayer cannot change God's will. I know it. Say that prayer ten thousand times comes back like a stone. Yes, but Christ prayed, therefore I may and I will pray. Not only so, but I *must* pray; the wish felt and not uttered before God, is a prayer. Speak, if your heart prompts, in articulate words, but there is an unverbalized wish, which is also prayer. You cannot help praying if God's spirit is in yours.

Do not say I must wait until this tumult has subsided and I am calm. The worst storm of spirit is the time for prayer; the agony was the hour of petition. Do not stop to calculate improbabilities. Prayer is truest when there is most of instinct and least of reason. Say, "My Father, thus I fear and thus I wish. Hear thy foolish, erring child. Let this cup pass from me."

Erroneous Views of Prayer

Wrong notions are contained in that conception which He made negative, "As I will."

A common popular conception of prayer is that it is the means by which the wish of man determines the will of God. This conception finds an exact parallel in those anecdotes with which Oriental history abounds in which a sovereign gives to his favorite some token on the presentation of which every request must be granted. For example, Ahasuerus promised Queen Esther that her petition should be granted, even to the half of his kingdom. Also, Herod swore to Herodias' daughter that he would do whatever she should require. It will scarcely be said that this is a misrepresentation of a very common doctrine, for they who hold this misconception would state it this way and would consider the mercifulness and privilege of prayer is that by faith we can obtain all that we want.

Now in the text it is said distinctly this is not the aim of prayer nor its meaning. "*Not* as I will." The wish of man does not determine the will of God. Try this conception by four tests.

1. Test it by its incompatibility with the fact that this universe is a system of laws. Things are thus rather than thus. Such an event is invariably followed by such a consequence. This we call a law. All is one vast chain from which, if you strike a single link, you break the whole. It has been truly said that to heave a pebble on the seashore one yard higher up would change all antecedents from the creation, and all consequents to the end of time. For it would have required a greater force in the wave that threw it there, a different degree of strength in the storm, a change of temperature all over the globe, and a corresponding difference in the temperaments and characters of the men inhabiting the different countries.

The result is that when a child wishes a fine day for the following day's excursion and hopes to have it by an alteration of what would have happened without his wish, he desires nothing less than a whole new universe.

It is difficult to state this in all its force except to men who are professionally concerned with the daily observation of the uniformity of the divine laws. But when the astronomer descends from his serene gaze upon the moving heavens, or when the chemist rises from contemplating those marvellous affinities, the proportions of which are never altered, realizing the fact that every atom and element has its own mystic number in the universe to the end of time, or when the economist has studied the laws of wealth and seen how fixed they are and sure, then for us to hear that it is expected that, to comply with a mortal's convenience or plans, God shall place this whole harmonious system at the disposal of selfish humanity, seems little else than impiety against the Lord of law and order.

2. Test it next by fact.

Ask those with spiritual experience. We do not ask whether prayer has been efficacious; of course, it has been. It is God's ordinance. Without prayer the soul dies. But we ask whether the good derived has been that prayer brought them the very thing they wished for? For instance, did the plague come and go according to the laws of prayer or according to the laws of health? Did it come because men neglected prayer, or because they disobeyed those rules which His wisdom has revealed as the conditions of salubrity? And when it departed, was it because a nation lay prostrate in sackcloth and ashes, or because it arose and girded up its loins and removed those causes and those obstructions which, by everlasting law, are causes and obstructions? Did the catarrh or the consumption go from him who prayed, sooner than from him who humbly bore it in silence? Try it by the case of Christ–Christ's prayer did not succeed. He prayed that the cup might pass from Him. It did not so pass.

Now lay down the undeniable principle, "The disciple is not above his master, nor the servant above his lord. It is enough for the disciple that he be as his master, and the servant as his lord." What Christ's prayer was not efficacious to do, that ours is not certain to effect. If the object of petition is to obtain, then Christ's prayer failed; if the refusal of His position did not show the absence of the favor of His Father, then neither does the refusal of ours.

Nor can you answer this statement by saying, "His prayer could not succeed because it was decreed that Christ should die, but ours may succeed because nothing hangs on our fate, and we know of no decree that is against our wish."

Do you mean that some things are decreed and some are left to chance? That would make a strange, disconnected universe. The death of a worm as well as your death and the hour and moment of both are all fixed as much as His was. *Fortune, chance,* and *contingency* are only words which express our ignorance of causes.

3. Test it by the prejudicial results of such a belief.
To think that prayer changes God's will gives unworthy ideas of God. It supposes our will to be better than His, the Unchangeable, the Unsearchable, the All-wise. Can you see the totality of things–the consequences and secret connections of the event you wish? If not, would you really desire the terrible power of infallibility in order to secure it?

Consider also the dangers of price and lazy inactivity resulting from the fulfillment of our desires as a necessity. Who does not recollect such cases in childhood when some curious coincidences with our wishes were taken for direct replies to prayer and made us fancy ourselves favorites of heaven, in possession of a secret spell. These coincidences did not make us more earnest, more holy, but rather the reverse. Careless and vain, we fancied we had a power which superseded exertion; we contemptuously looked down on others. Those were startling and wholesome lessons which came when our prayer failed, and threw our whole childish theory into confusion. It is recorded that favorite once received from his sovereign a ring as a mark of her regard, with a promise that whenever he presented that ring to her she would grant his request. He entered on rebellion, from a vain confidence in the favor of his sovereign.

Arrested and in prison he sent, by messenger, the ring to her, expecting amnesty. The ring which he sent to her was not delivered by his messenger, and he was executed. So would we rebel if prayer were efficacious to change God's will and to secure His pardon.

If we think that answered prayer is a proof of grace, we shall be unreasonably depressed and unreasonably elated–depressed when we do not get what we wish, elated when we do; besides, we shall uncharitably judge other men.

Two farmers pray. The one whose farm is on light land prayed for rain; the other, whose contiguous farm is on heavy soil, for fine weather. Plainly one or the other must come, and that which is good for one may be injurious to the other. If this be the right view of prayer, then the one who does not obtain his wish must mourn, doubting God's favor, or believing that he did not pray in faith. Two Christian armies meet for battle as Christian men on both sides pray for success. Now if victory is given to prayer, independent of other considerations, we are driven to the pernicious principle that success is the test of right.

From all false ideas the history of this prayer of Christ delivers us. It is a precious lesson of the Cross that apparent failure is eternal victory. It is a precious lesson of this prayer that the object of prayer is not the success of its petition, nor is its rejection a proof of failure. Christ's petition was not gratified, yet He was the one well-beloved of His Father.

The True Efficacy of Prayer

All prayer is to change the human will into submission to the divine will "as thou wilt." Trace the steps in this history by which the mind of the Son of Man arrived at this result. First, we find the human wish almost unmodified, that "the cup might pass from him." Then He goes to the disciples, and it would appear that the sight of those disciples, cold, unsympathetic, asleep, chilled His spirit, and set that train of thought in motion which suggested the idea that perhaps the passing of that cup was not His Father's will. In any case He goes back with this perhaps, "*If* this cup may not pass from me except I drink it, Thy will be done." He goes back again, and the words become stronger now: "Nevertheless not as I will, but as Thou wilt." The last time He comes, all hesitancy is gone. Not one trace of the human wish remains; strong in submission, He goes to meet His doom – "Rise, let us be going: behold he is at hand that doth betray me." This, then, is the true course and history of prayer. Hence we conclude:

1. That prayer which does not succeed in moderating our wish and in changing the passionate desire into still submission – is no true prayer, and such a prayer proves that we have not the spirit of true prayer.

Hence, too, we learn:

2. That life is most holy in which there is least of petition and desire and most of waiting upon God, that in which petition most often passes into thanksgiving. In the prayer taught by Christ there is only one petition for personal good, a singularly simple and modest one, "Give us this day our daily bread," and even that expresses dependence much more than anxiety or desire.

From this we understand the spirit of that retirement for prayer into lonely tops of mountains and deep shades of night of which we read so often in His life. It was not so much to secure any definite event as the need of holy communion with His Father—prayer without any definite wish; for we must distinguish two things which are often confounded. Prayer for specific blessings is a very different thing from communion with God. Prayer is one thing, petition is quite another. Indeed, hints are given us which make it seem that a time will come when spirituality shall be so complete, and acquiescence in the will of God so entire, that petition shall be superseded. "In that day ye shall ask me nothing" (John 16:23). "Again I say not I will pray the Father for you, for the Father Himself loveth you" (John 16:26,27). And to the same purpose are all those passages in which He disapproves of the heathen idea of prayer, which consists in urging, prevailing upon God. "They think that they shall be heard for their much speaking. Be not ye therefore like unto them: for your Father knoweth what things ye have need of, before ye ask Him" (Matthew 7:7,8).

Practically then, I say, Pray as He did, until prayer makes you cease praying. Pray until prayer makes you forget your own wish, and leave it or merge it in God's will. The divine wisdom has given us prayer, not as a means whereby we escape evil, but as a means whereby we become strong to meet it. "There appeared an angel unto Him from heaven, strengthening Him." That was the true reply to His prayer.

And so, in the expectation of impending danger, our prayer has won the victory, not when we have warded off the trial, but when, like Him, we have learned to say, "Arise, let us go to meet the evil."

Now contrast the moral consequences of this view of prayer with those which, as we saw, arise from the other view. By contrast, we learn that mistrust of our own understanding which keeps us from dictating to God. We also learn that benevolence which, when we contemplate the good of the whole rather than self-interest, dreads to secure what is pleasing to self at the possible expense of the general good. We learn that humility which looks on ourselves as atoms, links in a mysterious chain, and shrinks from the dangerous wish to break the chain. Finally, we learn the certainty that the All-wise is the All-good and that "all things work together for good" (Romans 8:28), for the individual as well as for the whole. Then, the selfish cry of egotism being silenced, we obtain Job's sublime spirit, "Shall we receive good at the hand of God, and shall we not receive evil?" (Job 2:10).

There is one objection that may be made to this. It may be said, if this is prayer, I have lost all I prized. It is sad and depressing to think that prayer will alter nothing and bring nothing that I wish. All that was precious in prayer is struck away from me.

But one word in reply. You have lost the certainty of getting your own wish; you have got instead the compensation of knowing that the best possible, best for you, best for all, will be accomplished. Is that nothing? Will you dare to say that prayer is no good at all unless you can reverse the spirit of your Master's prayer, and say, "Not as *Thou* wilt, but as *I* will?"

Where Our Greatest Battles Are Fought

John Henry Jowett (1864-1923) was known as "the greatest preacher in the English-speaking world." Born in Yorkshire, England, he was ordained into the Congregational ministry. His second pastorate was at the famous Carr's Lane Church, Birmingham, where he followed the eminent Dr. Robert W. Dale. From 1911-18, he pastored the Fifth Avenue Presbyterian Church, New York City; and from 1918-23, he ministered at Westminster Chapel, London, succeeding G. Campbell Morgan. He wrote many books of devotional messages and sermons. This message comes from *God – Our Contemporary*, published by Fleming H. Revell.

J.H. Jowett

5

WHERE OUR GREATEST BATTLES ARE FOUGHT

Men ought always to pray and not to faint (Luke 18:1).

THAT WORD was spoken when the Master's noontide was already past. The shadows were lengthening upon the way, and some of the Lord's sayings breathed the air of coming night. The road was heavy with deepening gloom, and now and again in the windings one caught the glimpse of a cross. The disciples were startled into confusion. The happenings ran against all their expectations. The things which the Master was speaking about were a brutal defiance of their fondest hopes. They had been looking for a golden harvest, and now the snow was falling. They had been eagerly anticipating the gaily colored dignities of dominion, and their eyes were now turned upon the black trappings of defeat. They had been stepping forward to a kingdom and to the shared sovereignties of a throne, and now a scaffold begins to loom at the end of the road. And so their minds were torn with uncertainties and distracted with doubt. Fear, too, came into their hearts with chilling menace, and some of them were tempted to retreat. Others became weary and heavy in their goings. Others again began to faint.

Constant Prayer

In our scriptural passage, we have a specific teaching of the Lord to be used against the assault of circumstances and the threat of impending doom. What is this specific teaching which makes one master of the changing way? "Men ought always to pray and not to faint." The guiding word may mean that men are always to pray and never to faint in prayer. Or it may mean that men ought always to pray and as a result, never faint even when antagonisms rear themselves like awful mountain ranges between them and their goal. It is probable that both interpretations are equally true and that both are included in the Master's mind and purpose. For the cardinal matter is the heavy emphasis which Jesus Christ puts upon the ministry of prayer as a predominant means of grace. "Men ought *always* to pray." The fellowship is to run through all the changing seasons of life, through spring and summer, and autumn and winter. We are "always to pray!" in the springtime of life when the blossoms are forming, in the winter when the snow is falling and the trees are bare! When we are sauntering through green pastures or toiling across the wilderness! Pray! In the playfield or in the battlefield! In the winsome dawn which sheds its light upon the marriage altar or in the empty darkness which gathers about the tomb. "Men ought *always* to pray." Such is the fervent pressure of the Master's word. And what He urged others to do He was always doing Himself. He prayed always. He prayed in the brilliant sunshine when the multitude would have taken Him by force and made Him a king. He prayed in the night in which He was betrayed—when all others had fled. He prayed in the open fields when He was feeding a famished crowd. He prayed by the grave of Lazarus. He prayed in the midst of the pestilence that walketh in darkness; He prayed in the midst of the destruction which wasteth at noon day. Most surely He exemplified the counsel which He gave to His disciples when He said that "Men ought always to pray."

Close Communion

Now let us consider one or two primary matters concerning this mighty business of prayer. And let us say first of all that the ministry of prayer is not entirely one with the exercise of petition. Prayer and petition are not synonyms, two names for the same thing. If the realm of prayer finds its symbol in some noble estate, then petition is like one field on the landscape. And there are seasons of prayer when we need not be in that particular field at all. Our spirit may be wandering in other parts of the wide domain. I am not disparaging the mighty prerogative of petition, but I am saying that it is only a part of our spiritual inheritance.

> Thou art coming to a King,
> Large petitions with thee bring.

Yes, I know it, and there are seasons when I would come to the King, burdened with intercessions, and I would spread the world of my necessities before the favor of His grace. I am coming to a King, but I am coming to more than a King. I am coming to a Father, and Fatherhood is larger than Kingship, just as home is larger than a throne. A king may have gifts at his disposal and may have honors and benefits and offices to confer upon his subjects, but fatherhood moves in a circle of intimacies and shared secrets, even in the matchless commerce of truth and grace and love. When prayer turns into this marvellous realm it is not so much a suppliant, laden with petition, as a wondering child walking in the revealing companionship of the Father in heaven. Prayer is not always like Lazarus, clothed in rags and bowing in suppliancy at the rich man's gate; it is sometimes like Lazarus in the Father's bosom, resting in the secret place of the Most High, and walking and talking in the shadow of the Almighty.

I may be pardoned for dwelling upon this distinction, as I think we are not always conscious of the range of the inheritance of the saints in light, and we only occupy a corner in our Father's house. I was once present at a prayer meeting, and one led us in prayer who was very evidently a disciplined traveler in the realms of grace. He left the field of petition, and he went wanderingly and wonderingly along among the unsearchable riches of Christ as though he were straying among the amazing glories of matchless woods. And the leader of the meeting bore with the traveler for some time and then broke out impatiently, "Brother, ask God for something! Ask God for something!" But the brother did not seem to have anything to ask for just then; it was quite enough to be walking with his Father in the boundless realms of grace. "Ask God for something!" No, prayer is not always petition, sometimes it is just communion. It is the exquisite ministry of friendship. It is the delicate passage of intimacies; it is the fellowship of the Holy Spirit.

Visual Meditation

Now let me state a second primary matter concerning this mighty business of prayer. If it is not always in the form of petition neither need it be always in the form of words. I want to try to say something which is very real to me, but which almost refuses the clumsy ministry of expression. There is a very vital part of prayer which can do without the vehicle of words. We can escape from the burden of the limitation of words. Who has not felt the bondage of speech, the cumbersomeness of words when he has sought to pray? And who has not experienced the peril of living words becoming dead forms? For me, there are times in prayer when I long to escape from the ministries of words, and to have wordless fellowship in the presence of God.

This is what I mean. First of all, we quietly and reverently put ourselves into the presence of God, we collect our scattered consciousness in the sense that God is near, and we come before His presence. How is the presence revealed? Who can say? Are there any means or methods which men and women have practiced in the realization of the presence of the unseen Friend? Yes, there are, but I suppose we must say that there are almost as many ways as there are people who have practiced them. Some call in the aid of a devout imagination, and in the secret place they realize a face, even the face which was unveiled to us in the Nazarene. To others the sacred Presence assumes no form, because there is no image which their consecrated imagination can frame which seems worthy of their unutterable devotion. Horace Bushnell led his spirit into a certain bright luminousness in which the presence of the Lord was veiled, and he communed with Him in the light. That is also the way of a very dear friend of mine who is greatly learned in the things of grace. His spirit withdraws in the presence of a shining splendor, and there he holds his fellowship. Others have nothing of this kind at all. They just recall themselves into God's presence, and without any image of form or any sense of light they know and feel that God is near. But these differences do not really matter, and it is well for everyone just to take the way which gives them the most intimate assurance of the presence of God.

Vital Interests Cared For

But I think it is not necessary for us to emphasize anyone's particular way as being the way for others. Never mind another's way, seek your own. Recall your spirit into the silence. You may not necessarily be in solitude; it may even be in the midst of a crowded train. Withdraw into the secret depths of your own spirit. Quietly say to yourself that the Eternal God, who revealed Himself in Jesus Christ our Lord, is near. You may be perfectly sure that you will become more expert in this sense of discernment as you continue in its practice. You will realize that you are in the presence of God. And now, as you realize it, introduce into that presence anything which concerns you and in which you have a vital interest. Let your imagination rest on that thing and quietly bring it to the sacred silence where you are closeted with God. See it clearly, and then, with great deliberateness, introduce it almost visibly into the sacred presence. That is to say you are now intelligently and imaginatively bringing some interests into the heavenly places, and you are setting it in the light of God. That is to say, you are thinking of something while your mind is suffused with the sense of God. You are bringing the two into fellowship and setting them face to face. You need not utter a word, but can escape from the crude bondage of your own ignorance and from the narrow limitations of speech. You offer no verbal petition, but you set your human concern in the mighty and pervasive influence of the Spirit of God. There must be no irreverent haste. There must be no frivolous tramping of the holy courts. It must all be done with patient deliberateness as you steadily hold the interest, whatever it might be, in the holy light of God. And no words are needful.

Suppose the vital interest be your own child. Well, then, set yourself in the sacred silence with a sense that you are near your Lord, and then, with alert imagination, bring your child into the holy place. See him there, hold him there. And what are you doing? You are establishing vital currencies between him and the divine presence, and you can do it without the ministry of words. Of course, you may speak if you will, but I think your words will be few. For in setting him there in the silence, you are praying, and you are presenting him to the grace and wisdom of God, and your dedicated homage is providing channels for the river of the water of life.

Or it may be some personal habit which constitutes your vital concern. Or it may be some particular piece of business. It may be some loss which you have suffered, or some great gain which you have made. It may be a bride. It may be a widow. It may be an orphan. It may be a people, a race or a tribe. It may be one of ten thousand things. I am urging you to practice this means of grace, in thus introducing your interests to the sacred presence of the Almighty. See them there, and hold them there, and whether it be with words or without words, whether in verbal devotion or in attitude and act, you are carrying out something of the Master's counsel when He said, "Men ought always"—in everything and everywhere-"to pray and not to faint."

Our Battles Won

Well now, it is in the field of prayer that life's critical battles are lost or won. We must conquer all our circumstances there. We must first of all bring them there. We must survey them there. We must master them there. In prayer we bring our spiritual enemies into the Presence of God and we fight them there. Have you tried that? Or have you been satisfied to meet and fight your foes in the open spaces of the world? If I am like Bunyan's pilgrim and encounter Apollyon on the exposed road and begin my warfare there, I shall be sadly beaten, and he will leave me bruised and broken by the way. My resource is to get him immediately into the field of prayer and engage him there.

I am, therefore, trying to say in the spiritual realm what Lord Fisher once said in the realm of material warfare. He said, "Compel your enemy to fight you on your own drill ground." Yes, indeed, and when we fight the world and the flesh and the devil on the drill ground of prayer, we have a certain victory. Let us bring our evil thoughts to the field of prayer. Let us drag our mean judgments to the field of prayer. Let us drive our ignoble purpose and our insane prejudices and our malicious practices and our tyrannical passions to the same field. Let us fight them on our own drill ground and slay them there. Men ought always to bring their evil antagonisms and difficulties into the presence of God. Force them into God's holy place and there fight and slay. Men ought always to pray, and they will not faint in the heaviest day.

Troubles Overcome

And on the same field of prayer we must bring our troubles, for we overcome them in the holy place. It very frequently happens that many of our troubles lose their fictitious stature when we bring them into the presence of the eternal God. They shrink when we set them in a large place. It is almost amusing how little things appear when they are set in confined and narrow spaces. Put them in a bigger field and they lose their alarming size. And there are many anxieties that look gigantic until we set them in the holy field of prayer in the presence of the Lord. Yes, and there are other things which seem enormous and overwhelming until we set them in infinite relations. Sometimes a grave seems so big that it appears to fill the world. There is nothing in the world but the grave. When we see it on the fields of communion and in the glory of the light of the risen Lord, captivity is led captive as death itself is buried in the eternal life of God. It is not our father's purpose that we should see our dead in cemeteries, but rather in the heavenly fields of the infinite love; and it is there that death loses its cold and cruel servitude. It is when we compel death to go with us on to the fields of divine communion that the grave is seen to be only a vestibule of the life indeed. "O death, where is thy sting? O grave, where is thy victory?" (1 Corinthians 15:55)

And even when some of our troubles remain, as indeed they will, it is on the fields of prayer that we get above them and assume and assert our sovereignty in the power of the risen Lord. We have a very familiar phrase which, I think, is very suggestive. We say, "Under the circumstances!" But why should we be under them? Why should we not be regnant above them? Why slaves and not masters? Why under and not above? It is on the field of prayer that we get our circumstances beneath our feet. "Thou shalt tread upon the lion and the adder, the young lion and the dragon shalt thou trample under feet" (Psalm 91:13). "Ye shall have power to tread on serpents" (Luke 10:19). "I keep under my body and bring it into subjection" (1 Corinthians 9:27). That is the purposed sovereignty which is ours in Christ. And we daily assume the sovereignty and we ride our enemies on the wonder-working fields of prayer. Said Lord Fisher, "Fight your enemy on your own drill ground." Very well, then, lead your troubles to those holy fields, and get above them in the emancipating grace of the Lord.

Humanity Blessed

But prayer has larger relationships than any of these. I cannot only bring my spiritual enemies onto the battle-field of prayer and slay them there. And I cannot only bring my troubles into the expansive realm of prayer and ride them as the Creator rides the storm. I can bring the burdens and necessities of humanity into the sacred presence, and in my own life I can become a point of vital contact between God and the human race. For I am not a unit of mankind, isolated and independent, a being of separated interests, self-centered and self-contained. I am just a fraction, a single member, a limb, a mere fragment of humanity, and I am indissolubly connected with it. The solidarity of the human race is inclusive of me, and I am a vital and indivisible part. The moral and spiritual blood of the race runs through me, and through me it circulates throughout humanity.

When, therefore, I commune with God in prayer I become a point of contact, an inlet through which the divine life flows into the veins and arteries of humanity. That is no idle figure of speech. Every man is an inlet through which clean or unclean energies pour into the general life-pool of the human race. We cannot help it. My points of contact determine the character of my contributions, and if my supreme contact is with God in the communion of prayer, I become an open channel through which the blessed influences flow into human fellowship for its eternal good. And so the prayer-ground is the common ground of racial enrichment. The hands that make contact with the battery direct the electrical dynamic to every fiber and tissue of the body. And hands that are uplifted in prayer are conductors of the divine dynamic to the general brotherhood of humanity. And therefore our Master counsels us to retire into the secret place.

In conclusion, create a sensitive quietness about your spirit. Realize the sacred presence. And then slowly and deliberately, in the holy place, present your helpmeets and your antagonisms, your privileges and your necessities, your banes and your pains, your laughter and your tears. And in your life the ancient miracle of grace shall again be wrought, for the Son of Righteousness shall arise upon you with healing in His wings.

The Energy of Prayer

William M. Clow (1853-1930) was born in
Scotland and educated in Auckland, New
Zealand, and Glasgow, Scotland. From 1881 to
1911, he pastored five churches in Scotland and
then joined the faculty of the United Free Church
College in Glasgow. He taught theology for
several years and closed his ministry as principal
of the college. *The Cross in Christian Experience*
and *The Day of the Cross* are two of his most
popular books. This sermon comes from *The
Secret of the Lord*, which was published in 1911 in
London by Hodder and Stoughton.

W.M. Clow

6

THE ENERGY OF PRAYER

And He said unto them, This kind can come forth by nothing but prayer (Mark 9:29).

THE SUN had risen upon the earth when Jesus came down from the mount. It was late morning when He, with His three disciples, reached the place of their retreat. In the East the day's activity begins with the dawn. He found the quiet spot of their rest invaded by an excited multitude. In the midst stood the other disciples humiliated and mortified by their failure to cast out the evil spirit which possessed the epileptic child. When He had healed the boy and the crowd had departed, His disciples asked Him privately, "Why could not we cast him out?" (Mark 9:28). Christ's reply touches one of the deepest mysteries of the religious life. "This kind can come forth by nothing but by prayer." It proclaims that prayer is a force in the universe and that the blessedness of mankind is bound up with the prayers of God's people. That seemed so difficult and transcendent a statement to the earlier transcribers of the Gospel that they added the words "and fasting" to Christ's brief saying. They conceived that this tremendous power could be received only after some stern and self-denying discipline of the body and the soul. In some versions, this ascetic gloss has been removed. Jesus declared that great things are wrought by prayer alone.

Moods About Prayer

Most men find themselves at different times in two sharply contrasted moods towards prayer. In one mood prayer is our easy, inevitable, and most natural speech. When a man is walking with God it is his irresistible impulse to speak with Him. When we are certain of God's presence, we do not hesitate to ask Him to work in us and for us and through us. Or when we are in the depths of sorrow or of shame, prayer is our almost involuntary cry. The severer studies of the anthropologists have proved that there is no land in which men do not call upon an unseen power in their want and fear and pain. Even though a man may ignore God when his boat is sailing on an even keel, when his heart is overwhelmed, he cries to be led to the rock that is higher than he. Prayer is always a necessity. At other times it becomes a delight.

But in the other mood, prayer becomes a mystery and an effort. The difficulties seem so dark and insuperable that our very breath is caught when we attempt to pray. So many petitions seem to remain unanswered. The reign of law in the universe seems so absolute that the mind cannot reach any certainty that an answer to prayer is even a possibility. Why should a weak and sobbing human cry check the stars in their courses? The most deadening and disheartening barrier lies in the moral difficulty. Why should a man have to pray to a loving and merciful God? A man that is a father does not wait 'til the child who is laying on a bed of pain cries out for his sympathy and his healing. A man that is merciful does not wait 'til he hears the bleat of his sheep which he has lost. When our poor human hearts love, they do not wait to be begged that they may supply the needs of their dear ones. Why should prayer on our part be the indispensable condition of the working of God? We may receive some answers to these and other questions which trouble us if we take up, as simply as possible, this deep word of Jesus. "This kind can come forth by nothing but by prayer."

How Is Prayer an Energy for God?

In the first place, *prayer makes us more deeply conscious of God.* In the rush and stress of life, and never more than in these days when the song of speed is on every man's tongue, we tend to lose a sure and clear consciousness of God. It is not that people disbelieve in God. The atheist is unknown. A generation ago he slipped back from the proud and defiant standpoint of the unbeliever to the more diffident position of the agnostic. Never was faith in God and a submission to the authority of Christ so unquestioning as today. But in this busy and engrossing world, when the mind is filled every morning with all the news of the ends of the earth, and the interest of the heart is held, as the eyes are held by a drama on the stage, God falls out of men's thoughts. If men will not sometimes think of God, He will merely become a name to them. If they glance toward Him only now and again, and with an unobservant and undesiring eye, He will become strange and shadowy and will remain unknown. We do not become sure of God by mustering up the arguments for His being and His purpose in the world. No heart ever stood up in a passionate conviction of God's presence because it had been told that His footprints were marked upon the rocks. No mind was ever driven by the logic of history to assent with a deep persuasion to the personal providence of the Almighty. These things have their place and their power. They are byways of evidence in which a believing heart will sometimes walk. But the only certainty which can satisfy the mind and stir the heart is an ethical and a religious, a moral and a spiritual consciousness of God.

Faith is an opening of the eyes that we may see. It is in prayer that we rise most swiftly and most convincingly into this faith which sees. It is in prayer that we have the sure consciousness of God. Even though a man may kneel with a haze over his mind and a chill upon his spirit, he will not kneel in vain. Sailors have called out of the mist and fog as their vessel has approached some hidden shore. They did not know how far off the cliffs were which were marked upon their chart. Still they called, and as the responding hail came back, they knew that eyes were watching and hearts were beating for them. In the same way men become sure of God when they pray to Him. Mark the result! To have a clear consciousness of God is to be filled with power.

In the second place, *prayer brings us into sympathy with the mind of God.* It is a sad commonplace that there are evils unnoticed, wrongs unremedied, poor unpitied and unhelped, miserable uncomforted, not because men do not know, but because they do not sympathize. Their eyes look out daily on scenes of poverty and of pain. Their ears are filled with the cries of those who suffer. But they do not seem to see or to hear because their hearts have not been touched to sympathy. Travellers in Africa all dwell on the callous way in which a band of bearers look upon one of their number who is carrying his load in utter exhaustion. They will leave him behind them on the trail, well aware that soon his bones will be bleaching in the sun. They will obey any command to care for him with a sulky discontent. They will meet the order to carry him almost with rebellion.

There was a day when Christians heard the cry from the regions beyond and yet gave it no heed. To this day people are told of the darkness and degradation, the fear and the whispering dread, the torture of body and of mind, the infamy of life and of spirit, all of which prevails over large tracts of Asia and of Africa, and they listen unmoved. The cries of children, the sobs of widowed hearts, and the sighs of over-driven men fall upon some men's ears as they take their ease and yet leave them cold. Ever and again some great soul rises who sees and hears with a new throb of sympathy. He sees right into the misery of the pain and wrong. He sees all the iniquity which is the spring of these bitter streams. With George Müller of Bristol and other like-minded men he hears the cry of the children. With William Carey and his long line of noble fellow-laborers he feels the burden of those who walk in darkness. With William Clarkson he is afflicted with the wrongs of the slave. He stands as a prophet of God to his generation. But what is the source of his sympathy? Whence came the light of his seeing? "With Thee is the fountain of life; and in Thy light we shall see light" (Psalm 36:9). Every one of these leaders in helping the oppressed have been men of prayer. As they have continued in prayer, they have come to learn the mind of Christ. They have begun to think His thoughts. They have become one with Him in spirit. He has lived and breathed within them. As the tide of sympathy with the mind of God has risen in their souls while they prayed, they were endued with the power of God.

In the third place, *prayer surrenders us to the energy of God.* The highest attitude in prayer is not desire nor aspiration nor praise. It is surrender. In surrender we open our whole being to God as a flower opens itself to the sun, and we are filled, up to our measure, with His divine energy. It is because man can be filled with the fulness of God that he has been chosen of God as His instrument in the world. In one true sense God set bounds to His power when He created man. He placed a further limit on Himself when He committed dominion to him. God now works through man, and if man will not work the works of God, the works of God remain undone. God might have peopled the world, as He has spread the stars through the heavens, by a word of command. He has chosen to people the world by one generation bringing forth another. If men will not replenish the earth, it will remain as lonely as a wilderness. He might have chosen to make the earth a place of order and beauty by the breath of His Spirit. But He has put man into His garden to till it. If a man will not take care of the garden it will become woods and prairie. He might have committed the gospel to a dispensation of angels, or have written His message in letters of light on the midnight sky, or made every stone breathe forth a Memnon music of appeal with every morning light. But He has committed to humans the ministry of reconciliation, and if they refuse to be God's ambassadors His gospel shall remain unknown.

There is a strange deep saying of the Old Testament in which a psalmist charges the Hebrew people with limiting the Holy One of Israel. We limit God when we think meanly of Him and teach men an impoverished doctrine of His grace. We limit God when we will not keep His commandments and do His will. We limit God by every act of rebellion which blocks His way. But there is one way in which we limit God most effectually of all. That way is by our prayerlessness. Because we are not surrendered to God in prayer, the might of His energy does not pass into us. Every faculty a man has, every talent God has given him, every fibre of his heart, and every cell in his brain may be energized by the energy of God. "He giveth power to the faint, and to them that have no might He increaseth strength" (Isaiah 40:29). People whom others have despised, teachers whom the strong have scorned, humble and lowly and unlearned men and women have done great things for God because they have been so surrendered to Him that His energy has been a swift dynamic in every faculty of body and of soul.

That truth is written in such large letters that one wonders why any man doubts the efficacy of prayer, or why so many men neglect it. It is always after ten days of prayer that Pentecost comes, and Peter stands up with new and amazing powers of exposition and of eloquence. In his surrender he has been filled with all the energy of God. We never come into close touch with any man who has lead a revival or been an instrument in the renewal of faith in multitudes of men, but we are impressed both by his personal weakness and his strange and mysterious strength. In his prayer of surrender he has been filled with the energy of God. The whole inwardness of this truth is written in the journal of John Wesley. For over twelve years he served in the ministry without power and without joy. But he came to that day when in prayer he surrendered himself and he was filled with the energy of God. His life thereafter was a daily yielding of himself to God. His journal, on almost every page, records his constant and daily touch with his Almighty Lover. On the first page of his diary he discloses the whole secret. He writes: "I resolved *Deo juvante*: 1) To devote an hour morning and evening to private prayer; no pretence or excuse whatever. 2) To converse with God; no lightness, no foolish talking. As with Wesley, all who receive God's potent energy in prayer do great things for God.

In the fourth place, *prayer works on the will of God.* No error has done more to paralyze our faith in prayer and to make the prayer of faith a wistful observance than the strange conception that God is fixed and inexorable law, if not even an iron and inflexible fate. There are many praying men who are fatalists in their heart. But God is not law, nor is He fate. God is will. The essential truth about will is this, that it is continually forming new plans, making fresh choices, and coming to unprophesied decisions. The common thought of God is that He is a personality bound hand and foot by His laws. The conception that lies behind much of the seemingly wise writing of many clever men is that God has no other laws than those we know and no higher methods than those we use. But God is a sovereign will with infinite resources. God's will as an eternal purpose in Christ cannot be finally thwarted. God's will as a fixed and steadfast purpose of grace shall be fulfilled. "I am the Lord, I change not" (Malachi 3:6). God is not a man that He should lie, neither the son of man that He should repent (Numbers 23:19). As Bunyan writes in his rustic couplet:

> Whether to heaven or hell you tend,
> God will have glory in the end.

God's will, as Jesus tells us in the prayer He taught us to pray, is not always done. It is not His will that one of the little ones should perish, and yet the sighs of their dying hours ascend to His throne. His will is our sanctification, and yet our sanctification is not an actuality. Men can thwart His intentions, check His plans, block His way, both within their own souls and in the outer world of life. A man can resist the Holy Spirit. As a man can thwart and check the will of God, so also can he move that will and work on it to his blessing and his help. As he brings his desires and his will to bear on the will of God, he moves God and alters His method and His ways. The issue is often seen in what men call miracles. But there are no miracles with God. Yet the answers to a human prayer are signs and wonders which seem to interrupt the course of nature, to divide the seas in their beds, and to keep the sun from going down.

This is the only scriptural conception of the will of God. Never did men guard so jealously against thinking of God as a man as did these Old Testament teachers. Yet they boldly say that God loves, fears, hopes, rejoices, grieves, repents of His methods, and changes His mode of dealing. With one voice they declare that God may be entreated, His anger turned away, and the course He has threatened left untravelled. Abraham does not doubt but that God can be turned aside from the destruction of Sodom. Moses does not doubt but that God can be led to take fresh pity on His disobedient people and keep their name in His book. Hezekiah is assured that the Lord will turn back the shadow of death. They are well aware that the whole truth lies in an infinite mystery beyond their power to fathom. But this they know, that their prayers are not empty and idle breath, but forces which can act on the mind and will of God. This they are confident of, that a man can wrestle with God and can prevail.

The New Testament Scripture is equally emphatic in its testimony. Jesus is most daring of all, when again and again He urges men to persistent praying which has power to change even the expressed mind of God. The urgent praying that Jesus demands in the bringing of the whole force of an eager will, in sympathy with God's inner purpose, to bear upon His will and His ways.

So then – pray! When your child is lying on a bed of sickness, and wise eyes look on him with a pitying hopelessness, still – pray! When weakness has smitten you, and you have the sentence of death in yourself, still-pray! When your business affairs are in confusion, and there seems no relief from disaster and shame, still-pray! When the heart of a once noble people seems to have become gross, and their ears are deaf to every appeal, still – pray! Who can tell whether God will be gracious to you.

However, it may not be His will to grant your prayers. Your request may conflict with His eternal purpose of grace. He is the moral governor of the universe, and your request may stand right in the way of wisdom, if not of mercy and love. He is your Father, but He has a spiritual purpose towards you which may require the denial of much that seems to you your necessary good. He cannot grant all the prayers of His children, any more than you can grant all the prayers of yours. He may answer their purpose when He may seem to deny their request. He did not grant Abraham's prayer for Sodom, but He answered the heartthrob in it when He sent His angels to lay their hands on the wrists of Lot. He did not answer the prayers of the stricken hearts of Israel when they saw the days of the captivity coming upon them. But the enriching years of exile were a better gift than centuries of unblessed and unenlightened prosperity in Jerusalem. He did not grant Christ's appeal in Gethsemane, "Let this cup pass from Me." He gave Christ His cross. But He made the cross Christ's cup of delight for evermore. Prayer has power with the will of God.

"This kind can come forth by nothing save by prayer." Christ's words lie clearly in the light. Had these disciples been deeply conscious of God, had they been in sympathy with His mind, had they been surrendered to the inflow of His energy, and had they, in prayer, moved His will, they would have cast out the evil spirit from the epileptic child. They were impotent because they were prayerless. Yet we need not be at God for every trifle. The life of prayer we must always live. But there are wrongs we can redress, there are diseases we can heal, there are broken hearts we can comfort, by means God has placed already in our power. He has given us our talents and our aptitudes; He has given us His word of truth and His grace. He has given us our eyes, and our hands, and our voices, and our renewed and tender hearts. These we can use for Him. But when it comes to casting out the devils of people's hate, greed and sensual desire, and to the exorcising of the dark passions of the mutinous human heart—"this kind can come forth by nothing save by prayer." In this deadly strife it is Moses, with the upheld hands, and not Joshua, who wins the victory.

Jesus On Prayer

David Martyn Lloyd-Jones (1895-1981) was
trained to be a doctor. But he felt a call to the
ministry in 1927 and accepted a Presbyterian
church in his native Wales. G. Campbell Morgan
hand-picked Lloyd-Jones to succeed him at
Westminster Chapel, London; and "the Doctor's"
strong expository ministry drew large
congregations, particularly to the Friday Night
Bible Class. Calvinistic in doctrine and classically
Puritan in his homiletical style, Lloyd-Jones has
left an indelible mark on preachers and preaching
in the twentieth century. This message is chapter
2 of *Studies in the Sermon on The Mount* (vol. 2),
published 1959 by Wm. B. Eerdmans Company.

D. Martyn Lloyd-Jones

7

JESUS ON PRAYER

IN MATTHEW 6:5-8, we come to an example taken by our Lord to illustrate His teaching concerning piety or the conduct of the religious life. This is the theme which He considers in the first eighteen verses of this chapter. "Take heed," He says in general, "that ye do not your righteousness before men, to be seen of them: else ye have no reward with your Father which is in heaven." Here is His second illustration of this. Following the question of almsgiving comes the whole question of praying to God, our communion and our fellowship with God. Here, again, we shall find that the same general characteristic which our Lord has already described is, alas, far too much in evidence. This portion of Scripture, I sometimes think, is one of the most searching and humbling in the entire realm of Scripture.

But we can read these verses in such a way as really to miss their entire point and teaching, and certainly without coming under conviction. The tendency always when reading this is just to regard it as an exposure of the Pharisees, a denunciation of the obvious hypocrite. We read, and we think of the kind of ostentatious person who obviously is calling attention to himself, as the Pharisees did in this matter. We therefore regard it as just an exposure of this blatant hypocrisy without any relevance to ourselves. But that is to miss the whole point of the teaching here, which is our Lord's devastating exposure of the terrible effects of sin upon the human soul, and especially sin in the form of self and of pride.

Sinful Attitudes

Sin, He shows us here, is something which follows us all the way, even into the very presence of God. Sin is not merely something that tends to assail and afflict us when we are far away from God, in the far country as it were.

Sin is something so terrible, according to our Lord's exposure of it, that it will not only follow us to the gates of heaven, but – if it were possible – into heaven itself. Indeed, is not that the Scripture teaching with regard to the origin of sin? *Sin is not something which began on earth.* Before man fell there had been a previous Fall. Satan was a perfect, bright, angelic being dwelling in the heavenlies; and he had fallen before ever man fell. That is the essence of the teaching of our Lord in these verses. It is a terrible exposure of the horrible nature of sin.

Nothing is quite so fallacious as to think of sin only in terms of actions; and as long as we think of sin only in terms of things actually done, we fail to understand it. The essence of the biblical teaching on sin is that it is essentially a *disposition.* It is a *state of heart.* I suppose we can sum it up by saying that sin is ultimately self-worship and self-adulation, and our Lord shows (what to me is an alarming and terrifying thing) that this tendency on our part to self-adulation is something that follows us even into the very presence of God. It sometimes produces the result that even when we try to persuade ourselves that we are worshipping God, we are actually worshipping ourselves and doing nothing more.

That is the terrible nature of His teaching at this point. This thing that has entered into our very nature and constitution as human beings is something that is so polluting our whole being that when people are engaged in their highest form of activity they still have a battle to wage with it. It has always been agreed, I think, that the highest picture that you can ever have of a person is to look at him on his knees waiting upon God. That is the highest achievement of man; it is his noblest activity. Man is never greater than when he is there in communion and contact with God. Now, according to our Lord, sin is something which affects us so profoundly that even at that point it is with us and assailing us. Indeed, we must surely agree on the basis of New Testament teaching that it is only there we really begin to understand sin.

We tend to think of sin as we see it in its rags and in the gutters of life. We look at a drunkard, poor fellow, and we say: There is sin; that is sin. But that is not the essence of sin. To have a real picture and a true understanding of it, you must look at some great saint, some unusually devout and devoted man. Look at him there upon his knees in the very presence of God. Even there, self is intruding itself, and the temptation is for him to think about himself, to think pleasantly and pleasurably about himself, and really to be worshipping himself rather than God. That, not the other, is the true picture of sin. The other is sin, of course, but there you do not see it at its acme; you do not see it in its essence. Or, to put it in another form, if you really want to understand something about the nature of Satan and his activities, think of that wilderness where our Lord spent forty days and forty nights. That is the true picture of Satan where you see him tempting the very Son of God.

All that comes out in this statement. Sin is something that follows us even into the very presence of God.

Necessary Rebirth

Before we come to our analysis of this, I would make one other preliminary observation which seems to me to be quite inevitable. If this picture does not persuade us of our own utter sinfulness, of our hopelessness as well as our helplessness, if it does not make us see our need of the grace of God in the matter of salvation, and the necessity of forgiveness, rebirth, and a new nature, than I know of nothing that ever can persuade us of it. Here we see a mighty argument for the New Testament doctrine about the absolute necessity of being born again, because sin is a matter of disposition, something that is so profound and so vitally a part of us that it even accompanies us into the presence of God.

But follow that argument beyond this life and world, beyond death and the grave, and contemplate yourself in the presence of God in eternity for ever and ever. Is not the rebirth something which is a bare essential? Here, then, in these instructions about piety and the conduct of the religious life, we have implicit in almost every statement this ultimate New Testament doctrine of regeneration and the nature of the new man in Christ Jesus.

Indeed we can go on even beyond that and say that even if we are born again, and even if we have received a new life and a new nature, we still need these instructions. This is our Lord's instruction to Christian people. It is His warning to those who have been born again; even they have to be careful lest in their prayers and devotions they become guilty of this hypocrisy of the Pharisees.

Two Ways of Praying

First, then, let us take this subject in general before coming to a consideration of what is commonly called "the Lord's Prayer." We are looking merely at what we might call an introduction to prayer as our Lord teaches it in these verses, and I think that once more the best way of approaching the subject is to divide it into two sections. There is a *false way of praying* and there is a *true way of praying*. Our Lord deals with them both.

False Way

The trouble with the false way is that its very approach is wrong. Its essential fault is that it is concentrating on *itself*. It is the concentrating of attention on the one who is praying rather than on the One to whom the prayer is offered. That is the trouble, and our Lord shows that here in a very graphic and striking way. He says: "When thou prayest, thou shalt not be as the hypocrites are: for they love to pray standing in the synagogues and in the corners of the streets, that they may be seen of men." They stand in the synagogue in a prominent position; they stand forward.

You remember our Lord's parable of the Pharisee and the publican who went into the temple to pray. He makes exactly the same point there. He tells us that the Pharisee stood as far forward as he could in the most prominent place, and there he prayed. The publican, on the other hand, was so ashamed and full of contrition that "standing afar off" he could not even so much as lift up his face to heaven, but just cried out, "God be merciful to me a sinner." In the same way our Lord says here that the Pharisees stand in the synagogues and in the corners of the street, in the most prominent position, and pray in order that they may be seen of men. "Verily I say unto you, They have their reward."

According to our Lord, the reason for their praying in the street corners is something like this. A man on his way to the temple to pray is anxious to give the impression that he is such a devout soul that he cannot even wait until he gets to the temple. So he stands and prays at the street corner. For the same reason, when he reaches the temple, he goes forward to the most prominent position possible. Now what is important for us is to extract the principle, so I put that as the first picture.

The second is put in the words: "When ye pray, use not vain repetitions, as the heathen do: for they think that they shall be heard for their much speaking." If we take these two pictures together, we shall find that there are *two main errors* underlying this whole approach to God in prayer. The first is that *my interest, if I am like the Pharisee, is in myself* as the one who is praying. The second is that *I feel that the efficacy of my prayer depends upon my much praying or upon my particular manner of prayer.* Let us look at these separately.

First Error – Showing Off

The first trouble, then, is this danger of *being interested in myself as one who prays.* This can show itself in many different ways. The first and the basic trouble is that such a person is anxious to *be known among others as one who prays.* That is the very beginning of it. He is anxious to have a *reputation* as a man of prayer, anxious and ambitions is that respect. That in itself is wrong.

The next step in this process is that it becomes a positive and actual desire *to be seen praying by others.* That, in turn, leads to things which will ensure that others do see us. This is a most subtle matter that is not always

blatant and obvious. There is a type of person who pa-
rades himself and puts himself in a prominent position
and is always calling attention to himself. But there are
also subtle ways of doing this self-same thing.

The biographer, who was anxious to show the saintliness of an author, illustrated it like this. "Nothing was
quite so characteristic of him," he said, "as the way in
which, when he was walking from one room to another,
he would suddenly in the corridor fall down on his knees
and pray. Then he would get up and go on his way again."
That, to the biographer, was proof of the saintliness and
devoutness of this particular man.

I do not think I need explain what I mean. The trouble
with the Pharisees was that they tried to give the impression that they could not wait until they got to the temple;
they had to stand where they were at the street corners to
pray, at once both blatant and obvious. Yes, but if you fall
down on your knees in a corridor in a house, it is rather
wonderful! I want to show on the basis of our Lord's
teaching that that man would have been a greater saint
if he had not dropped on to his knees, but rather had
offered up his prayer to God as he was walking along that
corridor. It would have been an equally sincere prayer,
and nobody would have seen it. How subtle this is!

"Enter into thy closet, and . . . shut thy door." My
prayer is always going to be the secret prayer. Yes, but it
is possible for a man to pray in secret in such a way that
everbody knows he is praying in secret, because he gives
the impression that by spending so much time there he is
a great man of prayer.

Of course, we must not be overscrupulous about these
matters, but the danger is so subtle that we must always
bear it in mind. I remember people talking about a man
who attended certain conferences and remarking with
great admiration that they noticed that he always
slipped away after the meetings, climbed a high rock
away from everybody else, and then got down on his
knees and prayed. Well, that good man certainly did
that, and it is not for me to judge him. But I wonder
whether in that great effort of climbing there was not a

little admixture of this very thing our Lord here denounces. Anything that is unusual ultimately calls attention to itself. If I go out of my way, metaphorically, *not* to stand at the street corners, but become famous as the man of the lonely rock, I may be calling attention to myself. That is the trouble; the negative becomes the positive in a very subtle manner before we realize what we are doing.

But let us follow it a little further. Another form which this takes is the terrible sin of praying in public in a manner which suggests *a desire to have an effect upon the people present rather than to approach God with reverence and godly fear.* I am not sure, for I have frequently debated this matter with myself, and therefore speak with some hesitance, whether all this does not apply to the so-called "beautiful prayers" that people are said to offer. I would question myself whether prayers should ever be beautiful. I mean that I am not happy about anyone who pays attention to the form of the prayer. I admit it is a highly debatable question and commend it to your consideration. There are people who say that anything that is offered to God should be beautiful and that, therefore, you should be careful about the phrasing and the diction and the cadence of your sentences. Nothing, they say, can be too beautiful to offer to God.

I admit there is a certain force in the argument. But it does seem to me that it is entirely negated by the consideration that prayer is ultimately a talk, a conversation, a communion with my Father; and one does not address one whom one loves in this perfect, polished manner, paying attention to the phrases and the words and all the rest. There is surely something essentially spontaneous about true communion and fellowship.

This is why I have never believed in the printing of so-called pulpit prayers. Of course, it ultimately rests on very much larger issues into which we cannot now enter. I am simply raising the question for your consideration. I would suggest, however, that the controlling principle is that the whole being of the person praying should be intent upon God and should be centered upon Him and that he should be oblivious to all other things. Far from desiring people to thank us for our so-called beautiful prayers, we should rather be troubled when they do so. *Public prayer should be such that the people who are praying silently and the one who is uttering the words should be no longer conscious of each other, but should be carried on the wings of prayer into the very presence of God.*

I think if you compare and contrast the eighteenth and nineteenth centuries in this respect you will see what I mean. We do not have many of the recorded prayers of the great evangelists of the eighteenth century, but we have many of the popular prayers of the so-called pulpit giants of the nineteenth century. I am not at all sure but that it was not just there that the change took place in the life of the Christian church, which has led to the present lack of spirituality and the present state of the Christian church in general. The church became polished and polite and dignified, and the supposed worshippers were unconsciously occupied with themselves and forgetful that they were in communion with the living God. Such forgetfulness is a subtle thing.

Second Error – Attention on Form

The second trouble in connection with this wrong approach arises when we *tend to concentrate on the form of our prayers, or on the amount or length of time spent in prayer.* "When ye pray," He says, "use not vain repetitions, as the heathen do: for they think that they shall be heard for their much speaking." You are familiar with what is meant by this term "vain repetitions." It is to be seen still in practice in many Eastern countries where they have prayer wheels. The same tendency is shown also in Roman Catholicism in the counting of beads. But again it comes to us in a much more subtle way.

There are people who often attach great importance to having a set time for prayer. In a sense it is a good thing to have a set time for prayer, but if our concern is primarily to pray at the set time rather than to pray, we may as well not pray. We can get so easily into the habit of following a routine and forgetting what we are really doing. As the Mohammedan at certain hours of the day falls down on his knees, so many people who have their set time for prayer rush to God at this particular time and often lose their tempers in doing so should anyone hinder them. They must get on their knees at this particular hour. Regarded objectively, how foolish it seems! But again, let every one examine himself.

It is not only the question of the set time, however; the subtle danger shows itself in yet another way. Great saints, for instance, have always spent *much time* in prayer and in the presence of God. Therefore we tend to think that the way to be a saint is to spend much time in prayer and in the presence of God.

But the important point about the great saint is not that he spent much time in prayer. He did not keep his eye on the clock. He knew he was in the presence of God; he entered into eternity as it were. Prayer was his life, he could not live without it. He was not concerned about remembering the length of time. The moment we begin to do that, it becomes mechanical and we have ruined everything.

What our Lord says about the matter is: "Verily I say unto you, they have their reward." What did they desire? They wanted the praise of men, and they had it. And similarly today they are spoken of as great men of prayer; they are spoken of as those who offered wonderful, beautiful prayers. Yes, they get all that. But, poor souls, it is all they will get. "Verily I say unto you, They have their reward."

Approaching God the Right Way

Let us turn from them to the true way. There is a right way of praying, and again *the whole secret is in the matter of the approach.* That is the essence of our Lord's teaching.

"Thou, when thou prayest, enter into thy closet, and when thou hast shut thy door, pray to thy Father which is in secret; and thy Father which seeth in secret shall reward thee openly. But when ye pray, use not vain repetitions, as the heathen do: for they think that they shall be heard for their much speaking. Be not ye therefore like unto them: for your Father knoweth what things ye have need of, before ye ask him" (Matthew 6:6-8).

What does it mean? When it is stated in terms of the essential principle, the one thing that is important when we pray anywhere is that *we must realize we are approaching God.* That is the one thing that matters. It is simply this question of "recollection," as it is called. If only we would realize that we are approaching God, everything else would be all right.

Process of Exclusion

But we need a little more detailed instruction, and fortunately our Lord gives it. He divides it up like this. First of all there is the process of *exclusion.* To make sure that I realize I am approaching God, I have to *exclude certain things.* I have to enter into that closet. "When thou prayest, enter into thy closet, and when thou hast shut thy door, pray to thy Father which is in secret." Now what does this mean?

There are some people who would fondly persuade themselves that this is just a prohibition of all prayer meetings. They say, "I do not go to prayer meetings, I pray in secret." But it is not a prohibition of prayer meetings. It is not a prohibition of prayer in public, for that is taught of God and commended in the Scriptures. There are prayer meetings recorded in the Scriptures, and they are of the very essence and life of the Church. That is not what He is prohibiting.

The principle is that there are certain things which we have to shut out whether we are praying in public or praying in secret. Here are some of them.

You shut out and forget other people. Then you shut out and forget *yourself.* That is what is meant by entering "into thy closet." You can enter into that closet when you are walking alone in a busy street or going from one room to another in a house. You enter into that closet when you are in communion with God and nobody knows what you are doing.

There is no value in my entering into the secret chamber and locking the door if the whole time I am full of self and thinking about myself and am priding myself on my prayer. I might as well be standing at the street corner. No; I have to exclude myself as well as other people; my heart has to be open entirely and only to God. I say with the Psalmist: "Unite my heart to fear thy name. I will praise thee, O Lord my God, with all my heart" (Psalm 86:11-12). This is of the very essence of this matter of prayer. When we pray we must deliberately remind ourselves that we are going to talk to God. Therefore other people, and self also, must be excluded and locked out.

The Need For Awe

The next step is *realization*. After exclusion, realization. Realize what? *Well, we must realize that we are in the presence of God.* What does that mean? It means realization of something of who God is and what God is. Before we begin to utter words we always ought to say to ourselves: "I am now entering into the audience chamber of that God, the almighty, the absolute, the eternal and great God with all His power and His might and majesty, that God who is a consuming fire, that God who is 'light and in whom is no darkness at all,' that utter, absolute Holy God. That is what I am doing." We must recollect and realize all that.

But above all, our Lord insists that we should realize that, in addition, He is our Father. "When thou hast shut thy door, pray to thy Father which is in secret; and thy Father which seeth in secret shall reward thee openly." The relationship is that of Father and child, "for your Father knoweth what things ye have need of, before ye ask him." O that we realized this! If only we realized that this almighty God is our Father through the Lord Jesus Christ. If only we realized that we are indeed His children and that whenever we pray it is like a child going to its father! He knows all about us; He knows our every need before we tell Him.

As a father cares for his child, looks at his child, is concerned about his child, and anticipates his needs of the child, so is God with respect to all those who are in Christ Jesus. He desires to bless us very much more than we desire to be blessed. He has a view of us; He has a plan and a program for us; He has an ambition for us—I say it with reverence—which transcends our highest thought and imagination. We must remember that He is our Father. The great, the holy, the almighty God is our Father. He cares for us. He has counted the very hairs of our head. He has said that nothing can happen to us apart from Him.

Then we must remember what Paul puts so gloriously in Ephesians 3:20. That He "is able to do exceeding abundantly above all that we ask or think." That is the true notion of prayer, says Christ. You do not go and just turn a wheel. You do not just count the beads. You do not say: "I must spend hours in prayer, I have decided to do it and I must do it." *You do not say that the way to get a blessing is to spend whole nights in prayer, and that because people will not do so they cannot expect blessing.* We must get rid of this mathematical notion of prayer. What we have to do first of all is to realize who God is, what He is and what our relationship to Him is.

The Need for Trust in God

Finally we must have *confidence.* We must come with the simple confidence of a child. We need a child-like faith. We need this assurance that God is truly our Father, and therefore we must rigidly exclude any idea that we must go on repeating our petitions because it is our repetition that is going to produce the blessing. God likes us to show our keenness, our anxiety, and our desire over a thing. He tells us to "hunger and thirst after righteousness" (Matthew 5:6) and to seek it; He tells us to "pray and not to faint" (Luke 18:1), we are told to "pray without ceasing" (1 Thessalonians 5:17). Yes; but that does not mean mechanical repetitions; it does not mean believing that we shall be heard for our "much speaking."

It means that when I pray I know that God is my Father, that He delights to bless me, that He is much more ready to give than I am to receive, and that He is always concerned about my welfare. I must get rid of this thought that God is standing between me and my desires and that which is best for me. I must see God as my Father, who has purchased my ultimate good in Christ and is waiting to bless me with His own fullness in Christ Jesus.

So, we exclude, we realize, and then in confidence we make our requests known to God, knowing He knows all about it before we begin to speak. As a father delights that his child should come repeatedly to ask for a thing rather than that the child should say, "Father has always done this," as the father likes the child to keep on coming because he likes *the personal contact*, so God desires us to come into His presence. But we must not come with doubtful minds; we must know that God is much more ready to give than we are to receive. The result will be that "thy Father which seeth in secret shall reward thee openly." O the blessings that are stored at the right hand of God for God's children. Shame on us for being paupers when we were meant to be princes; shame on us for so often harboring unworthy, wrong thoughts of God in this matter. It is all due to fear, and because we lack this simplicity, this faith, this confidence, this knowledge of God as our Father. If we but have that, the blessings of God will begin to fall upon us and may be so overwhelming that with D.L. Moody we shall feel that they are almost more than our physical frames can bear, and cry out with him, saying, "Stop, God."

God is able to do for us exceeding abundantly above all that we can ask or think. Let us believe that and then go to Him in simple confidence.

The Power of Prayer

Reuben Archer Torrey (1856-1928) is best
remembered for his association with D.L. Moody
and his ministry as superintendent of the Moody
Bible Institute of Chicago (1889-1908). He was
educated at Yale and did graduate study in
Germany. A powerful evangelist who preached
sermons with strong biblical content, Torrey
made several world tours and saw thousands
come to Christ under his ministry. He pastored
the Church of the Open Door in Los Angeles, CA,
and also served as dean of the Bible Institute of
Los Angeles (BIOLA). He wrote many books on
biblical themes and practical Christian service.
This sermon is taken from the volume *The Power
of Prayer*, published by Fleming H. Revell.

R.A. Torrey

THE POWER OF PRAYER

Ye have not, because ye ask not (James 4:2).

I BRING you a message from God contained in seven short words. Six of the seven words are monosyllables, and the remaining word has but two syllables and is one of the most familiar and most easily understood words in the English language. Yet there is so much in these seven short, simple words that they have transformed many a life and brought many an inefficent worker into a place of great power.

I spoke on these seven words some years ago at a Bible conference in central New York. Some months after the conference, I received a letter from the man who had presided at the conference, one of the best-known ministers of the gospel in America. He wrote me, "I have been unable to get away from the seven words on which you spoke at Lake Keuka, they have been with me day and night. They have transformed my ideas, transformed my methods, transformed my ministry." The man who wrote those words has since been the pastor of what is probably the most widely known of any evangelical church in the world. I trust that the words may sink into some of your hearts today as they did into his on that occasion and that some of you will be able to say in future months and years, "I have been unable to get away from those seven words, they have been with me day and night. They have transformed my ideas, transformed my methods, transformed my life, and transformed my service for God."

You will find these seven words in James 4:2, the seven closing words of the verse, "Ye have not, *because ye ask not.*"

The Secret of Christians Powerlessness

These seven words contain the secret of the poverty and powerlessness of the average Christian, of the aver-

age minister, and of the average church. "Why is it,"
many a Christian is asking, "that I make such poor
progress in my Christian life? Why do I have so little
victory over sin? Why do I win so few souls to Christ?
Why do I grow so slowly into the likeness of my Lord and
Savior Jesus Christ?" And God answers in the words of
the text: "Neglect of prayer. You have not, because you
ask not."

"Why is it," many a minister is asking, "that I see so
little fruit from my ministry? Why are there so few con-
versions? Why does my church grow so slowly? Why are
the members of my church so little helped by my ministry, and built up so little in Christian knowledge and
life?" And again God replies: "Neglect of prayer. You
have not, because you ask not."

"Why is it," both ministers and churches are asking,
"that the church of Jesus Christ is making such slow
progress in the world today? Why does it make so little
headway against sin, against unbelief, against error in
all its forms? Why does it have so little victory over the
world, the flesh, and the devil? Why is the average
church member living on such a low plane of Christian
living? Why does the Lord Jesus Christ get so little honor
from the state of the church today?" And, again, God
replies: "Neglect of prayer. You have not, because you
ask not."

The Early Church's Victory

When we read the only inspired church history that
was ever written, the history of the church in the days of
the apostles as it is recorded by Luke (under the inspiration of the Holy Spirit) in the Acts of the Apostles, what
do we find? We find a story of constant victory, a story of
perpetual progress. We read, for example, such statements as Acts 2:47: "The Lord added to the church daily
such as should be saved" and Acts 4:4: "Many of them
which heard the word believed; and the number of the
men was about five thousand," and Acts 5:14: "And believers were the more added to the Lord, multitudes both

of men and women." In addition Luke in Acts 6:7 states: "And the word of God increased: and the number of the disciples multiplied in Jerusalem greatly; and a great company of the priests were obedient to the faith."

And so we go on, chapter after chapter, through the twenty-eight chapters of Acts, and in every one of the twenty-seven chapters after the first, we find the same note of victory. I once went through the Acts of the Apostles marking the note of victory in every chapter, and without one single exception the triumphant shout of victory rang out in every chapter. How different the history of the church as here recorded is from the history of the church of Jesus Christ today. Take, for example, that first statement, "The Lord added to the church daily [that is, every day] such as should be saved." Why, nowadays, if we have a revival once a year with an accession of fifty or sixty members and spend all the rest of the year slipping back to where we were before, we think we are doing pretty well. But in those days there was a revival all the time and accessions every day of those who not only "hit the trail" but "were [really] being saved."

Why this difference between the early church and the church of Jesus Christ today? Someone will answer, "Because there is so much opposition today." Ah, but there was opposition in those days, most bitter, most determined, most relentless opposition in comparison with which that which you and I meet today is but child's play. But the early church went right on beating down all opposition, surmounting every obstacle, conquering every foe, always victorious, right on without a setback from Jerusalem to Rome, in the face of the most firmly entrenched and most mighty heathenism and unbelief. I repeat the question, "Why was it?" If you will turn to the chapters from which I have already quoted, you will get your answer.

Steadfast Prayer

Turn, for example, to Acts 2:42: "And they continued steadfastly in the apostles' doctrine and fellowship, in breaking of bread and in prayers." That is a picture very brief but very suggestive of the early church. It was a *praying church.* It was a church in which they prayed, not merely occasionally, but where they all "continued steadfastly . . . in prayers." They all prayed, not a select few, but the whole membership of the church; and all prayed continuously with steadfast determination. "They gave themselves to prayer," as the same Greek word is translated in Acts 6:4.

Now turn to Acts 6:4 and you will get the rest of your answer. "We will give ourselves continually to prayer." That is a picture of the apostolic ministry: it was a praying ministry, and a ministry that "gave themselves continually to prayer," or, to translate that Greek word as it is translated in former passage (Acts 2:42), "They continued steadfastly in prayer." *A praying church* and a *praying ministry!* Ah, such a church and such a ministry can achieve anything that ought to be achieved. It will go steadily on, beating down all opposition, surmounting every obstacle, conquering every foe, just as much today as it did in the days of the apostles.

Present-day Departure From Prayer

There is nothing else in which the church and the ministry of today or, to be more explicit, you and I have departed more notably and more lamentably from apostolic precedent than in this matter of prayer. We do not live in a praying age. A very considerable proportion of the membership of our evangelical churches today do not believe even theoretically in prayer. Many of them now believe in prayer as having a beneficial "reflex influence," that is, as benefiting the person who prays, a sort of lifting yourself up by your spiritual bootstraps. But as for prayer bringing anything to pass that would not have come to pass if we had not prayed, they do not believe in it, and many of them frankly say so, and even some of our "modern ministers" say so.

And with that part of our church membership that does believe in prayer theoretically – and thank God I believe it is still the vast majority in our evangelical churches – even they do not make the use of this mighty instrument that God has put into our hands that one would naturally expect. As I said, we do not live in a praying age. We live in an age of hustle and bustle, of man's efforts and man's determination, of man's confidence in himself and in his own power to achieve things, an age of human organization and human machinery, human push and human scheming, and human achievement, which in the things of God means no real achievement at all.

I think it would be perfectly safe to say that the church of Christ was never in all its history so fully, so skillfully and so thoroughly and so perfectly organized as it is today. Our machinery is wonderful; it is just perfect, but, alas, it is machinery without power; and when things do not go right, instead of going to the real source of our failure, our neglect to depend on God and look to God for power, we look around to see if there is not some new organization we can get up, some new wheel that we can add to our machinery. We have altogether too many wheels already. What we need is not so much some new organization, some new wheel, but "the Spirit of the living creature in the wheels" we already possess.

I believe that the devil stands and looks at the church today and laughs in his sleeve as he sees how its members depend on their own scheming and powers of organization and skillfully devised machinery. "Ha, ha," he laughs, "you may have your Boy Scouts, your costly church edifices, your multi-thousand-dollar church organs, your brilliant university-bred preachers, your high-priced choirs, your gifted sopranos and altos and tenors and bases, your wonderful quartets, your immense men's Bible classes, yes, and your Bible conferences, and your Bible institutes, and your special evangelistic services, all you please of them; it does not in the least trouble me, if you will only leave out of them the power of the Lord God Almighty sought and obtained by the earnest, persistent, believing prayer that will not take no for an answer." But when the devil sees a man or woman who really believes in prayer, who knows how to pray, and who really does pray, and, above all, when he sees a whole church on its face before God in prayer, "he trembles" as much as he ever did, for he knows that his day in that church or community is at an end.

Prayer has as much power today, when men and women are themselves on praying ground and meeting the conditions of prevailing prayer, as it ever has had. God has not changed, and His ear is just as quick to hear the voice of real prayer and His hand is just as long and strong to save as they ever were. "Behold, the Lord's hand is not shortened, that it cannot save: neither his ear heavy, that it cannot hear. But our iniquities may "have separated between us and our God, and "our sins have hid his face from you, that he will not hear" (Isaiah 59:1,2). Prayer is the key that unlocks all the storehouses of God's infinite grace and power. All that God is, and all that God has, are at the disposal of prayer. But we must use the key. Prayer can do anything that God can do, and as God can do anything, prayer is omnipotent. No one can stand against the one who knows how to pray and who meets all the conditions of prevailing prayer and who really prays. "The Lord God Omnipotent" works from him and works through him.

Prayer Will Promote Our Personal Holiness as Nothing Else, Except the Study of the Word of God

But what, specifically, will prayer do? We have been dealing in generalities; let us come down to the definite and specific. The Word of God very plainly answers the question.

In the first place, prayer will promote our personal piety, our individual holiness, our individual growth into the likeness of our Lord and Savior Jesus Christ as almost nothing else, as nothing else but the study of the Word of God. These two things, prayer and study of the Word of God, always go hand-in-hand, for there is no true prayer without study of the Word of God, and there is no true study of the Word of God without prayer.

Other things being equal, your growth and mine into the likeness of our Lord and Savior Jesus Christ will be in exact proportion to the time and to the heart we put into prayer. Please note exactly what I say: "Your growth and mine into the likeness of our Lord and Savior Jesus Christ will be in exact proportion to the time and to the heart we put into prayer." I put it in that way because there are many who put a great deal of time but so little heart into their praying that they do very little praying in the long time they spend at it.

On the other hand, there are others who, perhaps, may not put so much time into praying but put so much heart into praying that they accomplish vastly more by their praying in a short time than the others accomplish by praying in a long time. God Himself has told us in Jeremiah 29: 13: "And ye shall seek me, and find me, when ye shall search for me with all your heart."

We are told in Ephesians 1:3, that God "hath blessed us with every spiritual blessing in the heavenly places in Christ." That is to say, Jesus Christ by His atoning death and by His resurrection and ascension to the right hand of the Father has obtained for every believer in Jesus Christ every possible spiritual blessing. There is no spiritual blessing that any believer enjoys that may not be yours. It belongs to you now; Christ purchased it by His atoning death and God has provided it in Him. It is there for you; but it is your part to claim it, to put out your hand and take it. God's appointed way for claiming blessings by putting out your hand and appropriating to yourself the blessings that are procured for you by the atoning death of Jesus Christ is by prayer. Prayer is the hand that takes to ourselves the blessings that God has already provided in His Son.

Go through your Bible and you will find it definitely stated that every conceivable spiritual blessing is obtained by prayer. For example, it is in answer to prayer, as we learn from Psalm 139:23, 24, that God searches us and knows our hearts, tries us and knows our thoughts, brings to light the sin that there is in us and delivers us from it. It is in answer to prayer, as we learn from Psalm

19:12,13, that we are cleansed from secret faults and that God keeps us back from presumptuous sins. It is in answer to prayer, as we learn from the 14th verse of the same Psalm, that the words of our mouth and the meditations of our heart are made acceptable in God's sight. It is in answer to prayer, as we learn from Psalm 25:4,5, that God shows us His ways, teaches us His path, and guides us in His truth. It is in answer to prayer, as we learn from the prayer our Lord Himself taught us, that we are kept from temptation and delivered from the power of the wicked one (Matthew 6:13). It is in answer to prayer, as we learn from Luke 11:13, that God gives us His Holy Spirit. And so we might go on through the whole catalog of spiritual blessings and find that every one is obtained by asking for it. Indeed, our Lord Himself has said in Matthew 7:11: "If ye then, being evil, know how to give good gifts to your children, how much more shall your Father which is in heaven give good things to them that ask him."

One of the most instructive and suggestive passages in the entire Bible as showing the mighty power of prayer to transform us into the likeness of our Lord Jesus Himself, is found in 2 Corinthians 3:18: "But we all, with open face beholding as in a glass [The English Revision reads better, "reflecting as a mirror"] the glory of the Lord, are changed into the same image from glory to glory, even as by the Spirit of the Lord." The thought is that the Lord is the sun, you and I are mirrors, and just as a mischievous boy on a bright sunshiny day will catch the rays of the sun in a piece of broken looking-glass and reflect them into your eyes and mine with almost blinding power, so we, as mirrors, when we commune with God, catch the rays of His moral glory and reflect them out on the world "from glory to glory." That is, each time we commune with Him we catch something new of His glory and reflect it out on the world.

I'm sure you remember the story of Moses, how he went up into the mount and tarried about forty days with God, gazing on that ineffable glory, and caught so much of the glory in his own face that when he came down from the mount, though he himself did not know it, his face so shone that he had to draw a veil over it to hide the blinding glory of it from his fellow Israelites.

Even so we, going up into the mount of prayer, away from the world, alone with God, catch the rays of His glory, so that when we come down to other people, it is not so much our faces that shine (though I do believe that sometimes even our faces shine), but our characters, with the glory that we have been beholding. We then reflect out on the world the moral glory of God from "glory to glory," each new time of communion with Him catching something new of His glory to reflect out on the world. Oh, here is the secret of becoming much like God by remaining long alone with God. If you won't stay long with Him, you won't be much like Him.

One of the most remarkable men in Scotland's history was John Welch, son-in-law of John Knox, the great Scotch reformer; he is as well-known as his famous father-in-law, but in some respects a far more remarkable man than John Knox himself. Most people have the idea that it was John Knox who prayed, "Give me Scotland or I die." It was not, it was John Welch, his son-in-law. John Welch put it on record before he died that he counted that day ill-spent that he did not put seven or eight hours into secret prayer. When John Welch came to die, an old Scotchman who had known him from his boyhood said of him, "John Welch was a type of Christ." Of course, that was an inaccurate use of language, but what the old Scotchman meant was, that Jesus Christ had stamped the impress of His character on John Welch. When had Jesus Christ done it? In those seven or eight hours of daily communion with Himself. I do not suppose that God has called many of us, if any of us, to put seven or eight hours a day into prayer, but I am confident God has called most of us, if not every one of us, to put more time into prayer than we now do. That is one of the great secrets of holiness, indeed, the only way in which we can become really holy and continue holy.

Some years ago we often sang a hymn, "Take Time to Be Holy." I wish we sang it more in these days. It takes time to be holy, one cannot be holy in a hurry, and much of the time that it takes to be holy must go into secret prayer. Some people express surprise that professing Christians today are so little like their Lord, but when I stop to think how little time the average Christian today puts into secret prayer the thing that astonished me is, not that we are so little like the Lord, but that we are as much like the Lord as we are, when we take so little time for secret prayer.

Prayer Will Bring the Power of God Into Our Work

But not only will prayer promote as almost nothing else our personal holiness, but prayer will also bring the power of God into our work. We read in Isaiah 40:31: "They that wait upon the Lord shall renew their strength; they shall mount up with wings as eagles; they shall run, and not be weary; and they shall walk [plod right along day after day, which is far harder than running or flying], and not faint."

It is the privilege of every child of God to have the power of God in his service. And the verse just quoted tells us how to obtain it, and that is by "waiting upon the Lord." Sometimes you will hear people stand up in a meeting, not so frequently perhaps in these days as in former days, and say: "I am trying to serve God in my poor, weak way." Well, if you are trying to serve God in your poor, weak way, quit it; your duty is to serve God in His strong, triumphant way. But you say, "I have no natural ability." Then get supernatural ability.

The religion of Jesus Christ is a supernatural religion from start to finish, and we should live our lives in supernatural power, the power of God through Jesus Christ, and we should perform our service with supernatural power, the power of God ministered by the Holy Spirit through Jesus Christ. You say, "I have no natural gifts." Then get supernatural gifts. The Holy Spirit is promised to every believer in order that he may obtain the supernatural gifts which qualify him for the particular service to which God calls him. "He [The Holy Spirit] divideth to each one [that is, to each and every believer] severally even as he will" (1Corinthians 12:11). It is ours to have the power of God if we will only seek it by prayer in any and every line of service to which God calls us.

Are you a mother or a father? Do you wish power from God to bring your own children up in the "nurture and admonition of the Lord"? God commands you to do it and especially commands the father to do it. God says in Ephesians 6:4: "Ye fathers, provoke not your children to wrath: but bring them up in the nurture and admonition of the Lord."

Now, God never commands the impossible, and as He commands us fathers, and the mothers also, to bring our children up in the nuture and admonition of the Lord, it is possible for us to do it. If any one of your children is not saved, the first blame lies at your own door. Paul said to the jailer in Philippi: "Believe on the Lord Jesus Christ, and thou shalt be saved, and thy house" (Acts 16:31).

Yes, it is the solemn duty of every father and mother to have every one of their children saved. But we can never accomplish it unless we are much in prayer to God for power to do it. In my first pastorate I had as a member of my church a most excellent Christian woman, but she had a little boy of six who was one of the most incorrigible youngsters I ever knew in my life. He was the terror of the community. One Sunday, at the close of the morning service, his mother came to me and said: "You know–?" (calling her boy by his first name).

"Yes," I replied, "I know him." Everybody in town knew him.

"Yes," I replied, "I know he is not a very good boy." Indeed, that was a decidedly euphemistic way of putting it; in point of fact he was the terror of the neighborhood.

Then this heavy-hearted mother said, "What shall I do?"

I replied, "Have you ever tried prayer?"

"Why," she said, "of course I pray."

"Oh," I said, "that is not what I mean. Have you ever asked God definitely to regenerate your boy and expected Him to do it?"

"I do not think I have ever been as definite as that."

"Well," I said, "you go right home and be just as definite as that."

She went home and was just as definite as that, and I think it was from that very day, certainly from that week, that the boy was a transformed boy and grew up into fine young manhood.

Oh, mothers and fathers, it is your privilege to have every one of your children saved. But it costs something to have them saved. It costs your spending much time alone with God, to be much in prayer, and it costs also your making those sacrifices and straightening out those things in your life that are wrong; it costs the fulfilling the conditions of prevailing prayer. And if any of you have unsaved children, when you go home today get alone with God and ask God to show you what it is in your own life that is responsible for the present condition of your children. Straighten it out at once and then get down alone before God and hold to Him in earnest prayer for the definite conversion of each one of your children. Do not rest until, by prayer and by your putting forth every effort, you know beyond question that every one of your children is definitely and positively converted and born again.

Are you a Sunday school teacher? Do you wish to see every one of your Sunday school scholars converted? That is primarily what you are a Sunday school teacher for, not merely to teach Bible geography and Bible history, or even Bible doctrine, but to get the people in your class one and all saved. Do you want power from on high to enable you to save them? Ask God for it.

Examples of God's Power Evident in Prayer

When Mr. Alexander and I were holding meetings in Sydney, Australia, the meetings were held in the Town Hall, which seated about five thousand people. But the crowds were so great that some days we had to divide the crowds and have women only in the afternoon and men only at night. One Sunday afternoon the Sydney Town

Hall was packed with women. When I gave the invitation for all who would accept Jesus Christ as their personal Savior, surrender to Him as their Lord and Master, begin to confess Him as such before the world, and strive to live from this time on to please Him in every way from day to day, over on my left a whole row of eighteen young women of, I should say, about twenty years of age, arose to their feet. As I saw them stand side by side, I said to myself, "That is someone's Bible class." Afterwards they came forward with the other women who came to make a public confession of their acceptance of Jesus Christ. When the meeting was over, a young lady came to me, her face wreathed in smiles, and she said, "That is my Bible class. I have been praying for their conversion, and every one of them has accepted Jesus Christ today.

When we were holding meetings in Bristol, England, a prominent manufacturer in Exeter had a Bible class of twenty-two men. He invited all of them to go to Bristol with him and hear me preach. Twenty-one of them consented to go. At that meeting twenty of them accepted Christ. That man was praying for the conversion of the members of his class and was willing to make the sacrifices necessary to get his prayers answered. Revival would quickly come here in this city if every Sunday school teacher would go to praying the way they ought for the conversion of every scholar in his or her class!

Are you in more public work, a preacher perhaps, or speaking from the public platform? Do you long for power in that work? Ask for it.

Oh, men and women, if we would spend more nights before God on our faces in prayer there would be more days of power when we faced our congregations!

The Magnificence of Prayer

Alexander Whyte (1836-1921) was known as
"the last of the Puritans," and certainly his
sermons were surgical as he magnified the glory
of God and exposed the sinfulness of sin. He
succeeded the noted Robert S. Candlish as pastor
of free St. George's and reigned from that
influential Edinburgh pulpit for nearly forty
years. He loved to "dig again the old wells" and
share with his people truths learned from the
devotional masters of the past. His evening Bible
courses attracted the young people and led many
into a deeper walk with God. This sermon is taken
from Whyte's *Lord, Teach Us To Pray* (Hodder
and Stoughton, London, 1900), a book of twenty-
three remarkable messages on prayer.

Alexander Whyte

9

THE MAGNIFICENCE OF PRAYER

Lord, teach us to pray (Luke 9:11).
A royal priesthood (1 Peter 2:5).

"I AM [an] apostle," said Paul, "I magnify mine office" (Romans 11:13). And we also have an office. Our office is not the apostolic office, but Paul would be the first to say to us that our office is quite as magnificent as ever his office was. Let us, then, magnify our office. Let us magnify its magnificent opportunities, its momentous duties, and its incalculable and everlasting rewards. For our office is the "royal priesthood." And we do not nearly enough magnify and exalt our royal priesthood. To be "kings and priests unto God" – what a magnificent office is that!

But then, we who hold that office are people of such small and such mean minds – that our souls so decline and so cling to this earth – that we never so much as attempt to rise to the height and the splendor of our magnificent office. If our minds were only enlarged and exalted at all up to our office, we would be found of God far oftener than we are with our scepter in our hand and with our miter upon our head.

If we magnified our office, as Paul magnified his office, we could achieve as magnificent results in our office as ever he achieved in his. The truth is that Paul's magnificent results were achieved more in our office than in his own. It was because Paul added on the royal priesthood to the gentile apostleship that he achieved such magnificent results in that apostleship. And, if we would but magnify our royal priesthood as Paul did, it has not entered into our hearts so much as to conceive what God has prepared for those who properly perform their office as Kings and Priests unto God.

Prayer is the magnificent office it is because it is an office of such a magnificent kind. Magnificence is of many kinds, and magnificent things are more or less magnificent according to their kind. This great globe on which it strikes its roots and grows is magnificent in size when compared with that grain of mustard seed; but just because that grain of mustard seed is a seed and grows, that smallest of seeds is far greater than the great globe itself. A bird on its summer branch is far greater than the great sun in whose warmth she builds and sings because that bird has life and love and song, none of which the sun has in spite of its immensity of size, light, and heat.

A cup of cold water only, given to one of these little ones in the name of a disciple, is a far greater offering before God than thousands of rams and ten thousands of rivers of oil because there is charity in that cup of cold water. And an exclamation, a sigh, a sob, a tear, a smile, a psalm are far greater to God than all the oblations and incense and new moons and Sabbaths and calling of assemblies and solemn meetings of Jerusalem because repentance and faith and love and trust are in the sob and in that psalm.

And the magnificence of all true prayer – its nobility, its royalty, its absolute divinity – all stand in this, that it is the greatest kind of act and office that man, or angel, can ever enter on and perform. Earth is at its very best, and heaven is at its very highest, when men and angels magnify their office of prayer and of praise before the throne of God.

The Magnificence of God Is the Source and the Measure of the Magnificence of Prayer

"Think magnificently of God," said Paternus to his son. Now that counsel is the sum and substance of this whole matter. For the heaven and the earth, the sun and the moon and the stars, the whole opening universe of our day, the Scriptures of truth with all that they contain, the church of Christ with all her services and all her saints – all are set before us to teach us and to compel us indeed to "think magnificently of God." And they have all fulfilled the office of their creation when they have all combined to make us think magnificently of their Maker.

Consider the heavens, the work of His fingers, the moon and the stars, which He has ordained; consider the intellectual heavens also, angels and archangels, cherubim and seraphim; consider mankind also, made in the image of God; consider Jesus Christ, the express image of His person; consider a past eternity and a coming eternity, and the revelation thereof that is made to us in the Word of God and in the hearts of His people – and I defy you to think otherwise than magnificently of God. And, then, after all that, I equally defy you to forget, neglect, or restrain prayer. Once you begin to think aright of Him who is the Hearer of prayer and Who waits, in all His magnificence, to be gracious to you – I absolutely defy you to live any longer the life you now live.

"First of all, my child," said Paternus to his son, "think magnificently of God. Magnify His providence; adore His power; frequent His service; and pray to Him frequently and instantly. Bear Him always in your mind; teach your thoughts to reverence Him in every place, for there is no place where He is not. Therefore, my child, fear and worship, and love God; first, and last, think magnificently of God."

Our Power in Prayer

"Why has God established prayer?" asks Pascal. And Pascal's first answer to his own great question is this. God has established prayer in the moral world in order "to communicate to His creatures the dignity of causality." That is to say, to give us a touch and a taste of what it is to be a creator. But then, "there are some things ultimate and incausable," says Bacon, that interpreter of nature. And whatever things are indeed ultimate to us, and incausable by us, them God "hath put in His own power."

But there are many other things, and things that far more concern us, that He communicates to us to have a hand in of cause and creation. He does not give these opportunities under the full control of our own rash and hot hand nor at our precipitate and importunate will, but always under His holy hand and under the tranquility of His holy will. We hold our office and dignity of causality and creation under the Son, just as He holds His again under the Father.

But instead of that lessening our dignity, to us, it rather ennobles and endears our dignity. All believers are agreed that they would rather acknowledge that all things had their spring and rise and rule in the wisdom and the love and the power of God rather than in their own wisdom and love and power, even if they had the wisdom and the love and the power for such an office. But then, again, just as all believing men put on Jesus Christ to justification of life, so do they all put on, under Him, their royal robe and their priestly diadem and breast-plate, not as so many beautiful ornaments, beautiful as they are but as instruments and engines of divine power.

"Thus saith the Lord, the Holy One of Israel," – as He clothes His priests with salvation, – "Ask me of things to come concerning my sons, and concerning the work of my hand command ye me," (Isaiah 45:11). What a thing for God to say to man! What a magnificent office! What a more than royal dignity! What a gracious command and what a sure encouragement is that to pray! It is prayer for us, first, as His sons, – if His prodigal and dishonor-able sons, – and then for our fellows, even if they are as prodigal and as undeserving as we are.

Ask of Me! Even when a father is wounded and of-fended by his son, even then you feel sure that you have his heart strings in your hand when you go to ask him for things that concern his son, even though he is a bad son. Even when he sends you away in anger, his fatherly feelings are obvious to you as you depart, and he looks out his door to see if you are coming back to ask him again concerning his son. And when you become bold and venture back, he falls on your neck and says, "Command me all that is in your heart concerning my son."

Now, that is the "dignity of causality," that in which you are the cause of a father taking home again his son and the cause of a son saying, "I will arise and go to my father." That is your "magnificent office." That is your "royal priesthood."

The Real Riches in Prayer

And, then, there is this magnificent and right noble thing in prayer. Oh, what a noble God we have–says Pascal–that God shares His creatorship with us! And I will, to the praise and the glory of God this day, add this, that He makes us the architects of our own estates and the fashioners of our own fortunes. It is good enough to have an estate left us in this life if we forget we have it; it is good enough that we inherit a fortune in this world's goods if it is not our lasting loss. Only there is nothing great, nothing noble, nothing magnanimous or magnificent in that.

But to have begun life with nothing, and to have climbed up by pure virtue, by labor, and by self-denial, and by perseverance, to the very top,–this world has no better praise to give her best sons than that.

But there is a better world, of which this world at its best is but the scaffolding, the preparation, and the porch; and to be the architect of our own fortune in *that* world will be to our everlasting honor. Now, there is this magnificence about the world of prayer that in it we work out, not our own bare and naked and "scarce" salvation only, but undefilable, with all its unsearchable riches. Heaven and earth, time and eternity, creation and providence, grace and glory are all laid up in Christ; and then Christ and all His unsearchable riches are laid open to prayer; and then it is said to every one of us, "Choose you all what you will have, and command Me for it."

All God's grace and all His truth, have been coined–as Goodwin has it–out of purposes into promises; and then all those promises are made "Yea and amen" in Christ; and then out of Christ. They are published abroad to all people in the word of the Gospel; and then all these who read and hear the Gospel are put upon their mettle. For what a person loves, that he is. What a person chooses out of a hundred offers, you are sure by that choice who and what that person is.

And, accordingly, put the New Testament in any one hand and set the throne of grace wide open before him, and you need no omniscience to tell you that persons true value. If he lets his Bible lie unopened and unread, if he lets God's Throne of Grace stand till death, idle and unwanted, if the depth and the height, the nobleness and the magnificence, the goodness and the beauty of divine things have no command over him and no attraction to him—then you do not wish me to use words to describe the meanness of that persons mind. Look yourselves at what he has chosen; look and weep at what he has neglected and has forever lost!

But there are other people of a far nobler blood than that one is; there are great people, royal people; there are some people made of noble stuff and cast into a noble mold. And you will never satisfy or quiet those people with all you can promise them or pour out upon them in this life. They are people of a magnificent heart, and only in prayer have their hearts ever obtained full scope and a proper atmosphere. They would die if they did not pray. They magnify their office. You cannot please them better than to invite and ask them to go to their God in your behalf. They would go of their own notion and accord for you, even if you never asked them. They have prayed for you before you asked them, more than you know.

They are like Jesus Christ in this, and He will acknowledge them in this. While you were yet their enemies, they prayed for you and as good as died for you. And when you turn to be their enemies again, they will have their revenge on you at the mercy seat.

When you feel, somehow, as if coals of fire were—from somewhere—being heaped upon your head, it is from the mercy seat, where that magnanimous man is retaliating upon you. Now, Paul himself never magnified his office more or better than that. And it was in that very same way that our Lord magnified His royal priesthood when He had on His crown of thorns on the cross, when His shame covered Him as a robe and a diadem in the sight of

God, and when He interceded and said – "They know not what they do."

The Power of Secret Prayer

And then there is this fine and noble thing about prayer also, that *the acceptableness of it, and the power of it, are in direct proportion to the secrecy and the spirituality of it.* As its stealth is, as its silence is, as its hiddenness away with God is, as its unsuspectedness and undeservedness with men is, as its pure goodness and pure love and pure goodwill are – so does prayer perform its magnificent part when it is alone with God. The true closet of the true saint of God is not built of stone and lime. The secret place of God as well as that of people, is not a thing of wood and iron, and bolts and bars.

At the same time, Christ did say, shut your door. And in order to have the Holy Ghost all to himself and to be able to give himself up wholly – body, soul and spirit – to the Holy Ghost, the man after God's own heart in prayer always as a matter of fact builds for himself a little sanctuary, all his own; not to shut God in, but to shut out all that is not of God. He builds a house of God before he has as yet built a house for himself. You would not believe it about that man of secret prayer. When you see and hear him, he is the poorest, the meekest, the most contrite, and the most silent of men. As a result, you rebuke him because he so trembles at God's word.

If you could only see him when he is alone with the King! If you could only see his nearness and his boldness! You would think that he and the King's Son had been born and brought up together – such intimacies and such pass-words are exchanged between them. You would wonder, and you would not believe your eyes and your ears. If you saw him on his knees, you would see a sight. Look! He is in the audience Chamber. Look! He is in the Council Chamber now. He has a seat set for him among his peers. He is set down among the old nobility of the empire. The King will not put on His signet ring to seal a command till your friend has been heard. "Command

Me," the King says to him. "Ask me," He says, "for the things of my sons, command me things to come concerning them."

And as if that were not enough, that person of all prayer is still on his knees. He is "wrestling" on his knees. There is no enemy there that I can see. There is neither anything nor anyone that I can see near him, and yet he wrestles like a mighty man. What is he doing with such a struggle? Doing? Do you know what he is doing? He is moving heaven and earth. The man is removing mountains. He is casting this mountain, and that, into the midst of the sea. He is casting down thrones. He is smiting old empires of time to pieces. Yes, he is wrestling indeed! For he is wrestling now with God and now with man; now with death; and now with hell. See, the day breaks over his place of prayer! See, the Kingdom of God begins to come in on the earth! What a spot that is! What plots are hatched there! How dreadful this place is! Let us escape for our life out of it! Is that man, in there with God, your friend? Can you trust him with God? Will he speak about you when he is in audience? And what will he say? Has he anything against you? Have you anything on your concience or in your heart against him? Then I would not be you for the world! But no! Hear him! What is that he says? I declare I hear your name and your children's names! And the King stretches forth His scepter, and your friend touches it. He has "commanded" his God for you. He has "asked concerning" you and your sons. Such access, such liberty, such power, such prevalency, such magnificent office has he, who has been made of God a king and a priest unto God.

The Power of Humble People in Prayer

And, then, to cap and to crown it all—the supreme magnanimity, and the superb generosity of God, to its top perfection, is seen in this—in the people He selects, prepares for Himself, calls, consecrates, and clothes with the miter and with the ephod and with the breastplate. It is told in the Old Testament to the blame of Jeroboam, that "he made an house of high places, and made priests of the lowest of the people, which were not of the sons of Levi (1 Kings 12:31). But what is written and read in the Levitical Law to Jeroboam's blame, that very same thing, and in these very same words, God's saints are this Sabbath day singing in their thousands to His praise before the throne of God and the Lamb.

For, ever since the day of Christ, it has been the lowest of the people – those lowest, that is, in other men's eyes, and in their own – it has been the poor and the despised, the meek and the hidden, the down-trodden and the silent, who have had secret power and privilege with God and have prevailed. It was so, sometimes, even in the Old Testament. The New Testament sometimes broke into the Old, and in nothing more than in this in the men – and in their mothers – who were made kings and priests unto God.

"The Lord maketh poor," sang Samuel's mother, "and maketh rich: He bringeth low, and lifteth up. He raiseth up the poor out of the dust, and lifteth up the beggar from the dunghill, to set them among princes, and to make them inherit the throne of glory" (1 Samuel 2:7,8). And the mother of our great High Priest Himself sang, as she sat over His manger – "He hath regarded the low estate of His handmaiden... He hath filled the hungry with good things; and the rich hath He sent empty away" (Luke 1:48,53). This, then, is the very topmost glory, and the praise of God – the one from among humanity takes and makes of them kings and priests unto God.

Let all such people magnify their office, and let them think and speak and sing magnificently of their God!

A Pattern of Prayer

Alexander Maclaren (1826-1910) was one of
Great Britain's most famous preachers. While
pastoring the Union Chapel, Manchester
(1858-1903), he became known as "the prince of
expository preachers." Rarely active in
denominational or civic affairs, Maclaren
invested his time studying the Word in the
original and sharing its truths with others in
sermons that are still models of effective
expository preaching. He published a number of
books of sermons and climaxed his ministry by
publishing his monumental *Expositions of Holy
Scripture*. This message is taken from *Sermons
Preached in Manchester* (third series), published
1902 by Funk and Wagnalls Company.

Alexander Maclaren

10

A PATTERN OF PRAYER

Bow down thine ear, O Lord, hear me: for I am poor and needy.
Preserve my soul; for I am holy: O thou my God, save thy servant
that trusteth in thee. Be merciful unto me, O Lord: for I cry unto
thee daily. Rejoice the soul of thy servant: for unto thee, O Lord,
do I lift up my soul. For thou, Lord, art good, and ready to forgive;
and plenteous in mercy unto all them that call upon thee (Psalm
86:1-5).

"WHEN ye pray, use not vain repetitions, as the heathen
do" (Matthew 6:7). But earnest reiteration is not vain
repetition. The second is born of doubt; the first, of faith.
The prayer that springs from a deep felt need, and will
not cease till that need is supplied, may say the same
things over a hundred times and yet they shall not be
vain. Rather, as the same blood is repeatedly driven
through the veins by the contraction and dilating of the
heart, so all true prayer will flow forth over and over
again as the spirit opens in yearning and closes itself in
calm fruition on the grace it has received and then di-
lates again in longing and sense of need. So the Master,
who warned us against empty repetitions, enjoined upon
us the persistent prayer which prevails; and of Himself it
is written, "And he left them and went away again the
third time, saying the same words" (Matthew 26:44).

This faithful and prevailing reiteration remarkably
characterizes the striking series of supplications in the
text, Psalm 86:1-5. Substantially they are all one, but the
varying phases of the one wish show how familiar it was
in all its aspects to his mind, and the accumulation of
them is the token of his earnest longing and profound
sense of need. Like the great ancestor of his nation,
Jacob, he wrestles with God and prevails.

The psalm has quotations from earlier songs—especially David's. In all probability, then, we have here a

devout man in later ages, breathing out his cries to God and using, as we do, consecrated words of earlier Scripture, which he freely reproduces and blends with his own petitions. That is no sign of cold artificial prayer, any more than our petitions are to be so regarded because they often flow naturally in Bible words which are hallowed by many associations. Rather, in using them, we unite our poor lives with those of the saints of old who "cried unto the Lord in their trouble, and he saved them out of their distresses" (Psalm 107:13).

The fulness and variety of these petitions deserve careful consideration. My object now is mainly to bring out the richness of meaning which lies in them. Note the invocations, the petitions, and the pleas.

Calling on God

Is any part of our prayers, more formal, mechanical, unmeaning than our repetition of the name of Him to whom we speak? We round off sentences with it. We make beginnings of our prayers with it; we finish them conventionally, and properly, as we think, with it; but if we rightly understand the meaning of that element of the prayer which the old divines in their catechisms called an *invocation*, we shall understand that it is the foundation of all and that it professes very distinctly a faith which is anything but formal.

For when we call upon the name of God, if we do it correctly and come not under the condemnation of that commandment, "Thou shalt not take the name of the Lord thy God in vain"–what do we mean? What do we do thereby? Three things. We summon up before our thoughts that aspect of the divine character which lies in the name that we utter. We do not pronounce a mere syllable. We utter a significant word that tells us something concerning God, and when we use it, unless the majestic image which it is intended to flash into our mind does indeed sparkle and glow there, it would be better for us to be speaking in an unknown tongue than to have an unfruitful understanding.

Further, we profess that we are exercising an act of faith in the character as revealed in that name. We say in effect: "This aspect of thy divine all-sufficiency, this fragment of thine ineffable perfection, on this I build, and to this I make my appeal." Further, we bring before God His own character as a motive with Him. We say in effect: "I bring thee myself, and in that mighty name, for the sake of what it declares, I ask that these goods may be bestowed upon me." So, to call on God is to contemplate His character, to trust in that character which we contemplate, and to believe that He responds to the obligations that are involved therein.

If the foregoing then is the general idea of calling on God, we may now advance to notice how comprehensive and various are the names by which the psalmist calls upon his helper, God, and steadies his own confidence.

In general, this Psalm is remarkable for its frequent use of the divine names. In almost every verse they recur, and their frequency gives us a vivid impression of earnestness, of consciousness of need, and of faith so sore pressed that it could only sustain itself by perpetual renewal of its grasp of God. Five times in these verses of our text does he call on Him, and that by three different names—Jehovah, My God, Lord. These three sacred names have each a distinct meaning when used in prayer; they bring up aspects of the character of God as the basis of our confidence and the ground of our petitions.

He calls on *Jehovah*. As to that first name, let me remind you in the briefest possible way that it has a double force in Scripture—one derived from its literal, philological meaning, the other derived from its historical use and development. As concerns the former of these two, as we all know, I suppose, the word substantially implies eternal, timeless being, underived self-existence. His name is, "I am that I am," He who is and was and shall be, the one fontal source of all transitory and creatural life, who "himself unmoved moveth all things."

And, then, the name derives a force from the history of its origin in and use. It was given as the seal of the covenant, as the ground of the great deliverance from Egyptian bondage. The national existence rested upon it. The vitality of Israel was guaranteed by the eternity of Israel's God. The bush that burned and was not consumed was the emblem of Him who gives and is none the poorer, who works unwearied, who pours forth life and light through all ages to all creatures and diminishes no whit the fulness of the fountain of life which is with Him. And that undecaying, inexhausted being is the pledge of Israel's security, the guarantee that "He will not alter the thing that is gone out of His lips." It was the pledge and the basis of the great deliverance which made Israel a nation—it was a name that expressed God's purpose to form that people into His people, who should show forth His praise.

When we use it in our prayers, we contemplate and trust in and plead with Him with all these grand thoughts of eternal subsistence: inexhaustible power, unwearied strength, resources that never fail, purposes that never alter, a being that never fails, a nature lifted high above the mutations of time, who dwells in a region above all tenses and moods and *is*, and *was*, and *is to come* in one ineffable and mysterious present. Nor only so, but we likewise say, "and this rock of ages, the basis of all that is, has spoken and entered into the bonds of love and covenant with men, so that they can plead with Him His revealed character and appeal to Him on the ground of His ancient promise and begin all their believing petitions with that cry, 'O Jehovah, who livest for evermore; O Jehovah, the God of the covenant and the deliverer of thy people!'"

And, further, note the other name on which the psalmist rests both petitions and pleas, "O thou *my God.*" I need only remark that, so far as its own proper meaning is concerned, this name contains only what one might call the natural conception of divinity, as distinguished from the former, which is emphatically the name of the God of revelation. The word implies the abundance and fulness of power and so may be found, and often is found, on the lips of heathens. It contemplates the Almightiness rather than the moral attributes or covenant relations of God, as the ground of our hopes.

But then note how this general conception, which in itself does not travel beyond the idea common to all men of an unseen might throned in the heavens, becomes special on the psalmist's lips by the little word which he prefixes to it, *"my* God."

So far as we can judge from the Scriptures, it was David who first ventured to claim by that name the might of the God of Israel for *his. "My* God" is the token stamped upon David's psalms. The warmth of personal affection which throbs through them and the firmness of personal confidence are wonderfully expressed by that one word, which appropriates the strength and grace of the covenant for the solace of the single soul, "my".

Whether this psalm be his, or, as seems most probable, the work of a later lover of God, it is moulded after the type of his psalms. This second invocation of God derives its force from that one word which contemplates the unlimited strength and divine loftiness as completely possessed by and enlisted on the side of the poor soul that cries to Him. His bold and reverent hand stretches out to grasp the whole fulness of God. Thou art the God of Israel, the God of Abraham, and Isaac, and Jacob, the God of the whole earth – but thou art my God, mine for my faith, mine for my help.

Then, the final name which the psalmist here employs – *"Lord"* – is not, as a mere English reader might suppose, the same word as that which is rendered *"Lord"* in the first verse. That, as we have said, is Jehovah. This means just what our English word *lord* means; it conveys the general idea of authority and dominion. If you will observe, it is the most frequent name in this psalm. Its force on the psalmist's lips, and the thoughts which he associated with it, may be gathered from succeeding verses. "Among the gods there is none like unto thee, O Lord, neither are there any works like unto thy works," where incomparable elevation and supreme dominion are ascribed to Him. So, the psalmist goes on, "All nations whom thou hast made shall come and worship before thee, O Lord, and shall glorify thy name, for thou art great," where the thoughts of universal sovereignty and exaltation above all are deduced from that name. So, then, when we blend all these together, it is as if the psalmist had said, "The ever living, the covenant Jehovah, my God in whom I claim a personal interest, who loves me with an individualizing love, and cares for me with a specific care, the absolute monarch and sovereign of the whole universe is He to whom I come with my supplication. I think of His names, I trust in them, I present them to Him whom they all but partially declare; and I ask Him—for His own name's sake, because of what He is and hath declared Himself to be—to hear my poor cry, to answer my imperfect faith, to show Himself yet once again that which His name has from of old proclaimed Him to be."

For us to know and trust that name is the highest exercise of all faith. To utter it believing is the very essence of all true prayer. Not as a formal beginning and as a formal close, but as the only ground of acceptance, do we connect it with our petitions. It should begin our prayers as their foundation; it should end them as their seal.

The bare utterance of a name may be the purest formalism, or it may be the most intense faith. The deepest love often finds that all language fails and that to breathe the beloved name is enough. All tenderness may be put in it—all rapture, all praise. Do you remember the wonderful story of the resurrection morning: "Jesus saith unto her, Mary. She. . .saith unto him Rabboni?" (John 21:16). Her name on His lips was enough for unveiling His heart and revealing His person; His name on her lips was enough to express the confession of her faith, the eager rush of her spirit to Him, the outpouring of her heart, the ecstacy of her gladness that had died with Him and lived now, raised again from the dead.

Did any of you, parents, ever hear your child wake from sleep with some panic and shriek the mother's name through the darkness? Was not that a more powerful appeal than all words? And, depend upon it, that the soul which cries aloud to God, "the God and Father of our Lord Jesus Christ," though it have "no language but a cry," will never call in vain.

Petitions

We have examined our calling on God, and now we turn to the *petitions* which these verses give us. As I have said, they are all substantially the same, and yet they so vary as to suggest how familiar all the aspects of the deliverance that the psalmist desired were to him. We may discern, I think, a progress of thought through them, upon which I touch for a moment. The petitions are: "Bow thine ear," "hear me," "preserve me," "save thy servant," "be merciful unto me," "rejoice the soul of thy servant." There is, first, the cry that God would *hear*, the basis of all that follows. There is then a three-fold description of the process of deliverance: "preserve," "save," "be merciful." Then there is a longing for that which comes after the help, a consequence of the hearing: "Make the soul of thy servant glad."

It is very significant, and may teach us some lessons worth learning, that the psalmist, prior to all special supplication, begins with that cry—"Incline thine ear; hear me." "What!" you say, "does not God know everything?" Oh, yes, no doubt. And do you think that what I may call the cold, passionless, *natural* knowledge of omniscience is enough for our hearts? Something more goes to the "hearing" of prayer than the necessary omniscience of an infinite divine nature. There is an act of loving will, which is most clearly conveyed by that strong, and yet plain and intelligible, metaphor, "*Bow down* thine ear," as an eager listener puts his hand to his ear and bends the lobe of it in the direction of the sound.

He prays, too, in that petition, for what we may call hearing *embodied in an act* of deliverance. With God, to hear *is* to answer. As soon as we desire, He knows our longing; as soon as He knows our longing, He meets it with His gift. No appreciable time is occupied in the passage of the imploring message from earth to heaven, none in the return message of blessing from heaven to earth. As David says, in the grand psalm which recounts his deliverances, "My cry came before him, even into his ears. *Then* the earth shook and trembled" (Psalm 18:6-7). He hears when He lovingly regards our prayers; He hears when he mightily answers our cry—and these two are one.

The psalmist further prays for *acts of help and deliverance*: "Preserve my soul;" "save thy servant;" "be merciful unto me." These petitions are all substantially the same, but yet there are shades of difference between them which deserve notice. The first of them might be rendered, "guard" or "watch" my soul, and that rendering helps us to distinguish it from the others. Looking at all three, we see that the first prays for protection, the second goes a step further and prays for happy issue of that protection in safety, and the third digs deeper and prays for that mercy which is the sole foundation of both the protection and the safety which it ensures. God's guardianship achieves our salvation, and His saving guardianship is the fruit of His mercy.

While these three petitions then differ thus, in that they contemplate the process of our deliverance in its deepest root, in its patient, sedulous method, and in its happy end, they also differ in that they embody varying thoughts of the need and weakness of the suppliant. In the first two petitions he regards himself as defenseless and in peril. He needs a great hand to be cast around him, in the hollow of which he may be safe. His soul lies open to the assaults of foes like some little unwalled village in the plains, and he craves the garrison and guardianship of God's presence, the watchfulness of His unslumbering, omnipresent eye.

In the last petition, he thinks of himself as lowly and unworthy—for "mercy" is love shown to inferiors or to those who deserve something else. The consciousness of helplessness has become a consciousness of sin. Protection is not all that we need; there must be pardon too. That hand which is to be outstretched to guard and save might justly have been outstretched to smite. The sole ground of our confidence that God will be "our guard while troubles last" and will save us with a full salvation at the last is our trust that He will not refuse mercy to those who own their sin and seek forgiveness through Jesus Christ.

It is worth notice, too, that in all this variety of petitions for deliverance there is not a word about the exact manner of it. The way in which God's mercy is to guard and save is left, with meek patience, to God's decision. Let us not prescribe to Him the path which He shall take, but commit that to His own loving wisdom. There are two methods of lightening a burden—one is to diminish the load, the other is to strengthen the shoulders that carry it. The latter is often the more blessed—and often the shape in which God answers our prayer. "For this thing I besought the Lord thrice, that it might depart from me. And he said unto me, My grace is sufficient for thee" (2 Corinthians 12:8-9).

Then, in the final petition, the Psalm rises still higher and—not satisfied with imploring that God would hear, guard, and save—asks for gladness, too, "Rejoice the soul of thy servant."

We may venture to ask for and expect gladness if we are God's servants. All His creatures have a claim on Him for blessedness according to their capacity, so long as they stand where He has set them. And we who have departed from that obedience which is joy may yet, in penitent abasement, return to Him and ask that He would rejoice the soul of His servant. David's deepest repentance dared to ask, "Make me to hear joy and gladness that the bones which thou hath broken may rejoice" (Psalm 51:8). Our most troubled utterances of sore need, our sighs and groans, should be accompanied with faith which feels the summer's sun of joy even in the midwinter of our pain and sees vineyards in the desert.

We should believe in and hope and ask for more than bare deliverance—hard though it may be to think that gladness is any more possible. Blossoms and flowers will come again, even though untimely frosts have burned the young leaves into brown powder. No sorrow is so crushing and hopeless, but that happiness may again visit the heart where trust and love abide. Only let us remember that this psalm seeks for joy where it seeks to help, not from earthly sources but from God.

They who find their deliverance in God are often tempted to find their pleasure somewhere else. It is often easier to pray with tears, "Preserve me and save me," than with undistracted love to choose Him as our only delight. But the true devout heart turns equally to God for all its needs, and its prayer ever is, "Judge me, O God, and plead my cause . . . O deliver me . . . Then will I go unto the altar of God, unto God my exceeding joy (Psalm 43:1, 4).

Pleas

Finally, we have to consider the *pleas* on which these petitions are based.

The logic of prayer here is so remarkable and beautiful. Every feature of the psalmist's condition and character, as well as all that he knows of God, becomes on his lips a reason with God for granting his prayer. The same ingenuity of faith – if one might use such a phrase, which that Syro-Phoenician woman showed when she laid hold of the apparent rejection of her plea and gave back to Christ His own parable as a reason for His compliance-comes out here.

These pleas part into three. He pleads his *necessities*. He is "poor and needy," or rather, perhaps – giving a distinct meaning to each word – "afflicted and poor," borne down by the pressure of outward calamity and destitute of inward resources. So the one phase of our need is the evils that oppress us from without, and the other is the lack of power from within to bear up against these. Circumstances and character both constitute an appeal to God. Or, more simply, we are weighed upon with sore distress, and we are likewise deprived of all means either outside of us or within us.

Yes, Christian friends, by God's mercy we are emboldened to take our weakness, our helplessness, as pleas

with Him. We know how often the sight of misery touched the heart of Christ and how He was "moved with
compassion," and we believe that the compassion of
Christ is our truest image of the pity of our God. The
yawning emptiness of our parched hearts, thirsting for
God like the cracked ground during a drought, is a plea
with Him.

And when we draw near to His throne, we do not need
to present our merits but our necessities in order to
receive the answer. "Lord save, we perish" is our best cry
to awaken to energy the hand that never sleeps. Let no
consciousness of evil drive us from Him, but rather let it
impel us close to Him. The devil's lie is that we are too
bad to go to Him. The truth is that our necessities—yes
and our sins too—may be made pleas with Him. "Pardon
mine iniquity; *for it is great*" (Psalm 25:11).

He pleads his *relation to God* and his *longing for communion* with Him. "I am holy." That sounds strange.
There seems to be flavor of self-righteousness about it
which startles one. But there is no such thought in the
word, and the "holy" of the English version completely
obscures the psalmist's thought. It will be enough here to
say that the word of the original simply means "one who
is a recipient or object of mercy." It is passive, not active,
in signification. Of course the mercy meant is God's
mercy, so that the meaning is as our Bible has it in the
margin, "One whom thou favorest."

The plea then here is drawn, not from the righteousness of the man, but from the mercy of God. It sets forth
the relation between God and His suppliant from the
divine side, and pleads God's gracious bestowal of mercy
upon him in the past as a reason for its continuance and
perfecting. "Thou hast been pleased to love and favor me,
to enrich me with thy grace. Be what thou hast been: do
what thou hast done: forsake not the work of thine own
hands." And God, who begins no buildings which He is
not able to finish, recognizes the strength of the plea and
will perfect that which concerneth us.

There follows the same relation contemplated from the
human side, and that, too, is a plea with God. "Thy

servant that trusteth in thee." I am knit to Thee, as a servant I belong to Thy household, and the Master's honour is concerned in His dependent's safety. The slave is cared for by His Lord. I belong to Thee—do thou watch over what is thine own. I trust in Thee. We do not plead our faith as constituting a claim of merit with God, but as constituting a plea with Him. It is not that it deserves deliverance—else we might well hesitate to urge it, when we think of its weakness and often interruptions—but that it is sure to bring deliverance. For anything is possible rather than that the most tremulous trust should go unblessed and unanswered.

The human side of the relation between God and His servant is further urged in the subsequent clauses which refer to the Psalmist's longings and efforts after fellowship with God. "I cry unto thee daily"—he does not think that his cry deserves an answer, but he knows that in God's great mercy He has bound Himself to "hear our cry and save us", and he appeals to the faithful promise. He has put in practice the condition, and he expects the answer. It can only happen that he who calls on God will be answered. Anything is credible rather than that our prayer ascending should be flung back unanswered, as if it had struck against heavens which were brass. Let our faith clasp His promise, and then the fact of our prayer is with God a plea, and with us a pledge of His answer. Let us not doubt that we *do* wield power with God when we pray—and we shall prevail.

Again he pleads, "Unto thee do I lift up my soul." Such a plea expresses the conscious effort to raise his whole being above earth, to lift the heavy grossness of his nature, bound in the fetters of sense to this low world, up and up to the Most High, who is his home. And can it be that that yearning and striving after communion shall go unsatisfied? Is it possible that I shall stretch out feeling hands and grope in vain for God? Is it possible that He shall not take note of me, that my poor faith shall be disappointed, that my prayer shall be lost in empty space, that my soul shall not find its rest? Never. "What man is there of you, whom if his son ask bread, will he give him a stone? . . . How much more shall your father which is in heaven give good things to them that ask him?" (Matthew 7:9, 11).

And, finally, because our necessities and our desires derive their force as pleas from *God's own character*, he urges that as his last and mightiest appeal. He began with invocation, and he ends as he began. The name of God is the ground of all our hope and the motive for all His mercy. Turn away, Christian friends, from all thoughts of self, of your own needs, of your own trust, and prayer, and aspiration. Forsaking all other confidence, flee to that "name of the Lord" into which, as "a strong tower," we may "run and be safe." The one prevalent plea with God is the faithful recounting of all that grace and pity which He is exercising and has exercised. All others are subordinate and possess only a power bestowed by this. "For thou, Lord, art good, and ready to forgive; and plenteous in mercy unto all them that call upon thee." Our need is the occasion; faith and desire, the channel; but God is the reason and the source of all our deliverance and all our salvation. "Because he could sware by no greater, he sware by himself" (Hebrews 6:13)–and because we can pray by none other, we implore Him by Himself, for the sake of His own Holy Name, because He is that He is, to have mercy upon us who cry to Him.

And, friends, when *we* call on the name of Jesus Christ our Lord and ask that *our* prayers may be heard "for the sake of Christ," we are taking no other plea into our lips than that ancient and all prevalent one of this psalm. It is His own mercy in Christ which we present. It is the work of His own love which we bring as our plea. "I will declare thy name unto my brethren" (Psalm 22:22). Christ is the Revealer of the Father's name, and they who pray in the name of Christ have for their confidence this promise, "Whatsoever ye shall ask in my name, that will I do, that the Father may be glorified in the Son" (John 14:13)–and this, "Whatsoever ye shall ask the Father in my name, he will give it you" (John 16:23).

Prayer or Fainting

George Campbell Morgan (1863-1945) was the son of a British Baptist preacher and preached his first sermon when he was thirteen years old. He had no formal training for the ministry, but his tireless devotion to the study of the Bible helped him to become one of the leading Bible teachers of his day. Rejected by the Methodists, he was ordained into the Congregational ministry. He was associated with Dwight L. Moody in the Northfield Bible conferences and as an itinerant Bible teacher. He is best known as the pastor of Westminister Chapel, London (1904-17 and 1933-35). During his second term there, he had Dr. D. Martyn Lloyd-Jones as his associate. He published more than 60 books and booklets, and his sermons are found in *The Westminister Pulpit* (London, Pickering and Inglis). This sermon is from Volume 3.

G. Campbell Morgan

11

PRAYER OR FAINTING

They ought always to pray, and not to faint (Luke 18:1).

SUCH IS Luke's interpretation of the meaning of the parable which Jesus uttered to His disciples concerning the unrighteous judge "which feared not God, and regarded not man," but who granted the request of the importunate widow from the purely selfish motive which he expressed graphically and accurately in the words, "lest she wear me out by her continual coming." This is one of the most remarkable things in some senses that the Bible says anywhere about the prayer life, "They ought always to pray, and not to faint." It is one of those statements that stagger and in the presence of which Christian men and women are always in danger of indulging in some measure of that criticism which is the outcome of unbelief.

The first objection raised is to the word "always." It is suggested that this does not quite mean what it says, that the evident intention is that we should be men and women of prayer, having our appointed times and habits of prayer; that believing in the power of prayer, we ought to take advantage of the great possibility whenever we are able so to do, whenever we are in need. That is not what the text says. That is not the interpretation placed upon the parable of Jesus by Luke. The text says, *"always to pray."*

There are other passages that indicate the same necessity. When he is closing his letter to the Thessalonians Paul utters in epigrammatic form great injunctions concerning the Christian life. One of them is, "Pray without ceasing" (1 Thessalonians 5:17). Of this it is also affirmed that he did not literally mean that we are to pray without ceasing. We are to pray every day, two or three times a day, as regularly as possible. We are to be men and women of prayer. But that is not what the apostle wrote. He wrote, "Pray without ceasing." You will not at all misunderstand these introductory words.

I recognize the difficulty. You say, "I have been too busy today with work for God to take time in prayer. I was so pressed with the business cares of last week that I had very little time for prayer. I prayed at morning, noon, and night; and often in the midst of the city's rush and din, when some great need crowded on my heart, I lifted that heart to God. I prayed often, but I did not pray always; I did not pray without ceasing."

As a believer in the inspired infallibility of Scripture, I abide by the words of it, "*always,*" "*without ceasing.*" We are responsible, therefore, to ask very carefully what this text really means. I submit to you immediately that this particular text of mine in which Luke gives the inspired interpretation of the meaning of the Master's parable lifts the whole subject of prayer on to a very high level and reveals to us the fact that there is infinitely more in prayer than the offering of petitions, than the uttering of words, than the taking of time, than the attitude of the body or of the mind; that there are deeper depths and higher heights; and that if we would enter into the prayer life with all its fulness of virtue and of victory we must discover what this really means, "They ought always to pray," "Pray without ceasing."

For the Disciples

First of all, note the Authorized Version reads, "*Men* ought always to pray, and not to faint." The Revised Version reads, "*They* ought always to pray, and not to faint." To whom was *He* speaking? If you go back to the previous chapter (Luke 17) you will see how wonderful a chapter it is, full of solemn warnings and prophetic utterances, strange and mysterious many of them. At its twenty-second verse I find these words, "And He said unto the *disciples*, The days will come when ye shall desire to see one of the days of the Son of man, and ye shall not see it." Then He continues His teaching of the disciples right on to the end of that chapter, and immediately and in that connection, whether uttered at that point or not is of no consequence, in that relationship, according to the placing of the story by Luke, He spoke the parable "unto them," that is, to His own disciples, "that *they* ought always to pray, and not to faint." The distinction is an important one, and it is fundamental to our meditation. He had one philosophy of life, and He called on everyone to accept it. Here, however, He is laying His instructions upon such as have heard His call, and having obeyed it, have become His disciples. They are such as are described in Hebrews 11:6 – which I believe Luke wrote, although the thinking is the thinking of Paul – "He that cometh to God must believe that He is, and that He is a rewarder of them that seek after Him." If a man does not believe these things, he will never pray. If these things are indeed believed, if this is indeed the truth concerning God accepted by the heart and mind, then of such as believe, the Lord by His parable affirms that "they ought always to pray, and not to faint."

In Life's Stress

Having drawn attention to the fact that these words were spoken to disciples, to those who believe that God is and that He is a Rewarder, let us notice the circumstances of this discourse. He is talking to His disciples in view of the fact that the life of faith is a strenuous life, characterized by stress and strain and conflict and difficulty. Notice how He ends His exposition of His parable, "When the Son of man cometh, shall He find faith on the earth?" In the previous chapter I find Him telling these men that to gain their life they must lose it, and to find the real value of eternal things they must turn themselves away from all the allurements of the material and the sensual. He is putting into contrast the life of faith with the life that is lived on the material level.

Farther on, we notice that He said almost exactly the same thing. Speaking of the approaching destruction of Jerusalem and of the fact that in those days men would faint for fear, He charged His own to watch and make supplication. Thus, the message of this parable and the declaration of this text have application to such as are His disciples and declare to them the supreme truth concerning the secret of prevailing life in the midst of the stress and strain of discipleship.

I need hardly stay to argue the fact that the Christian life is one of stress and strain. I am perfectly well aware that there are senses in which it is a life of peace, ease, and quietness. I remember the great promises of Scripture concerning peace for the children of God. There is granted to the child of God the peace *from God* our Father. There is granted to the child of God the peace *of God* in the heart, and, moreover, the presence and comradeship of the *God of peace*.

Yet these very facts create the strain and stress and difficulty. Surrounded every day by things material, in the midst of an age which in its outlook is as absolutely godless as any age which has preceded it, it is not easy to live the life of godliness. It is not easy to bear perpetual and prevailing testimony to the unseen things to the ordinary crowd of men and women with whom the believer comes into contact, living, as they do, as though there were no God, no hereafter, no spiritual verities.

To live the life of godliness in the midst of this age is still to live the life of conflict. Because of the allied forces of godlessness, the Christian life is the strenuous life, and there are scores of men and women in this world tonight—perhaps the affirmation is a strong one, but I believe it to be true—who are weary in the midst of the Christian life, who are tired, fainting, and filled with weariness because of the pressure of the forces of the world upon them. To these people Christ says, "*They* ought always to pray, and not to faint."

The Meaning of Prayer

Before laying further emphasis upon the "always" let me take the terms of my text in order to understand Christ's philosophy of life for His own disciples. What is the real suggestiveness of this word "pray"? If you take it as to its first simplicity and intention, it means—and this is not complete, but it will help us to reach the complete thought—to wish forward, to desire toward the ultimate; or if you will have that interpreted by the language of the apostle in one of his greatest epistles, that to the Colossians (3:1), *it means the seeking of things which are above.* That does not at all suggest that the Christian is forevermore to be sighing after heaven, expressing discontent now with the present world, and longing to escape from it; but rather it means that the Christian is to seek the higher things, setting his mind upon them, and everywhere and all the time he is to be hoping for, and seeking to obtain, the ultimate. That is the simple meaning of prayer. Reaching forward, wishing forward, desiring forward, seeking the upper, the higher, the nobler.

Therefore, in prayer there is included, first, always first, the thought of worship and adoration, that content of the heart with the perfection and acceptability and goodness of the will of God which bows the soul in worship. That is the first attitude of prayer. To pray is now, always to set the life in its inspiration and in all its endeavor toward that ultimate goal of the glory of God. "Being justified by faith, let us have peace with God through our Lord Jesus Christ: through whom also we have access by faith into this grace wherein we stand, and *rejoice in hope of the glory of God*" (Romans 5:1-2).

The soul, seeing that golden age as in the will of God and realizing that the supreme fact of the vision is that of God Himself, the supreme attitude of the life is that of cooperation with God toward the ultimate upon which His heart is set. That is prayer.

Prayer is not merely position of body or of mind. Prayer is not merely asking for something in order that I may obtain it for myself. Prayer forevermore says when it asks for anything, "Not my will, but Thine be done," which means, if the thing I ask for, however much I desire it, however good it seems to me to be, will hinder or postpone by a hair's breadth or a moment, the ultimate victory, it should be denied to me. Those who know the real secret of the prayer life have discovered the fact that

God's denial of our requests is over and over again the graciousness of overwhelming answer. To pray is to desire forward, to seek forward to endeavor after. It is to have a new vision of God and of the ways of God, to be overwhelmingly convinced of the perfection of God, of the perfection of all He does and of the certainty of His ultimate victory, and then to respond to the profound and tremendous conviction by petition, by praise, and by endeavor; and so men "ought always to pray" and to "pray without ceasing."

The Meaning Of Fainting

Now notice another term of our text, "to faint". This is our Lord's recognition of the strenuous nature of the life of the believing soul. What is this word "to faint"? Quite simply, its meaning is *to be paralyzed, to be weak, to be worthless*, to feel the force dying and the vigor passing, to be beaten, to be broken down and helpless.

A Clear Choice

We may now consider our Lord's philosophy of life. He puts these two things into opposition. He declares in effect that this is the alternative before every one of us, to pray or to faint. There is no suggestion of a middle course. According to this word, this inspired interpretation of the meaning of our Lord's parable and teaching is, if men pray they do not faint. If men faint it is because they have ceased to pray. If men do not pray they faint. Men "ought always to pray, and not to faint." Interpret your prayer by the negation. Prayer is the opposite of fainting. Fainting is a sudden sense of inability and helplessness, the cessation of activity, weariness which is almost, and ultimately is, death. Pray and do not faint. To pray is to have the vision clear, the virtue mighty, the victory assured. To pray is to "mount up with wings as eagles," to "run and not be weary," to "walk, and not faint."

Pause with me one moment with that passage. Have you imagined that the great Isaiah at that point failed in his rhetorical method having said this great truth, he had nothing greater to say, and that afterward there was an anticlimax and perhaps something of pathos? It is not so. As a matter of fact, he began with the easiest thing of all to "mount up with wings as eagles." Then he took the next action in the order of difficulty, to run, and the hardest thing last, to walk.

In the day when you first caught your vision of God, you mounted up with wings of eagles. I am not undervaluing that day. Thank God for the experience. We thank God for it whenever it returns. He gives us the vision often, and we "mount up with wings as eagles." A defeated and disappointed man once said, "Oh, that I had wings like a dove! Then I would fly away and be at rest." What a mistake. A man with the wings of a dove could not fly away and be at rest. When the inspired seer speaks of a man flying, he says "wings as eagles." Notice the significance of it. The eagle is forevermore the symbol of deity. To wait upon God is to use the pinions of deity and mount and soar away.

Every young believer has those pinions and that great beginning, and God gives them to us throughout our pilgrimage. Presently, however, there comes a day when there are no wings and no mounting above; we must *run* through. Yet "they shall run, and not be weary." And yet there comes another day—some of you are in it now—when it is almost night, so dark has it all become. You cannot run, the way is not clear enough, the enemies are too many, there are difficulties all about you—you must walk, "They shall walk, and not faint." Notice Isaiah's word and Christ's, "They shall walk, *and not faint*," "They ought always to pray, and *not to faint*."

Prayer is the opposite of fainting. It is mounting with wings. It is running without weariness. It is walking the uphill, rough and rugged road, and never fainting. That is Christ's great philosophy of life. If men pray they do not faint. If men faint it is because they have forgotten to pray. "They ought always to pray, and not to faint."

God Versus the Unjust Judge

In the parable we notice it is an exposition of the philosophy of the prayer life by contract all the way through it. The moment you forget that, you miss the beauty and the glory of it. First, *all that the judge was, God is not.* The judge did not fear God, that is to say, he had not submitted to the highest authority. He did not regard men. He was absolutely careless, and you may sum up the whole thing in Christ's illuminative word, he was unrighteous. All that the judge was, God is not. God regards man. Notice the words of Jesus, "longsuffering over them." God is righteous. "He will avenge," and the word "avenge" there is not the word "revenge." It means to do justice to. The widow came to the unrighteous judge and said to him, "Avenge me of mine adversary. Do me justice in connection with my adversary." He was an unjust judge, an unrighteous man. God is righteous and just and will do justice by all who come to Him. That is the first contrast.

Another contrast. In order to persuade the unjust judge persistent pleading was necessary. Imploring is never necessary to persuade God. That is the point where we generally break down in this parable. We make the contrast between the unjust judge and God, but not between the consequent action of the widow and that of the Christian. This parable is constantly taken as teaching that we are to be persistent toward God. It teaches us rather that if we are always praying, praying in the sense of begging is not necessary. *The prayer life does not consist of perpetual repetition of petitions. The prayer life consists of life that is always upward and onward and Godward.* The passion of the heart is for the kingdom of God; the devotion of the mind is to His will; the attitude of the spirit is conformity thereto; and the higher we climb in the realm of prayer, the more unceasing will prayer be, and the fewer will be the petitions.

It is the opposite of fearful imploring that is taught here. Jesus describes God as compassionate, just, mighty, quick to respond to the forward wish of the weakest soul, so that in the midst of the stress and strain and struggle there need be no fainting. The life uplifted in prayer with the whole desire Godward brings an answer, and there is no comparison equal to showing the quickness of that answer. It is quicker than thought or the lightning flash.

There is a man here who is tired of his sin and broken-hearted on account of it, who determines that without any after-meeting he will seek the pardon of his God. Will he have to be importunate and wait and beg and beseech? No, God is "ready to pardon."

For example, imagine a great battleship, the decks are cleared for action, every man is at his post. At last, as the awful moment arrives, the commanding officer says, "Ready?" "Ready, yes, ready!" comes back the answer, and he gives the order, "Fire!" You know what happens. That is slow work compared to God's answer. He is ready to pardon, ready to answer your prayer.

The unjust judge did not regard God or man. He was selfish and self-centered. Because the widow went and went and went to him, to get rid of her, to save her bruising him, he gave her what she wanted. That is the picture by contrast. God is the opposite of that. Your method in prayer is the opposite of that. Therefore men "ought always to pray, and not to faint." Because of such a God, so full of compassion, so full of might, so full of infinite and strict integrity and justice, the foremost wish of the weakest, feeblest, frailest soul brings an answer. He is a God ready to hear and to answer.

The Duty and Power of Prayer

If all this is true, if this is what our Lord said to men, and if Luke's inspired interpretation of the meaning is correct, allow me for a moment to lay emphasis upon another word in the text, "They *ought* always to pray." It is a duty, not a privilege. Men ought. All omnipotence is at the disposal of the saint who prays since God is willing, then people ought to pray "Since God . . . pray so that they will not faint." There ought to be no fainting.

Oh, how strenuous is life! I know a little of it. Men "ought always to pray, and not to faint." How fierce the battle! I know something of the conflict, but I ought not to faint, because I can pray.

This truth means that in God there is a resource equal to every demand that can be made upon the trusting soul. There is no hour so dark but that if I will *stay upon Him* — once again to use Isaiah's fine language — I shall discover His readiness to support me as I stay. There is no battle so fierce but that if I pray I may not stand, withstand, . . . and, having done all, to stand (Ephesians 6:13). There is no temptation so swift, so sudden or subtle, but that if I am always praying I may not find at once the wisdom and the might that enable me to overcome. Men ought not to faint because men ought to pray.

How to Pray Always

The whole life of the believer should be prayer — and this is the summary and conclusion — every act, every word, every wish. The act that is not prayer in the ultimate, and the word which is not prayer in the last analysis, and the wish that is not prayer in the profoundest depth are to be put away; they do not become the life of faith. They are things that produce fainting.

How can every act be prayer? Ask yourself about your next act why you are doing it. The Sabbath will soon be over, and we shall leave it behind, for it is the day of prayer. Tomorrow morning you will face the calling of the day in the shop, the office, the school, professional life, — in whatever is your calling. What are you rising early and toiling all the day for? The answer of the average man will suit me for the moment. That answer will be, I am working for my living. Perfectly right, but what do you want to live for? Why should you endeavor to support your life and keep it? You have been overwhelmed with the stress and strain of actual physical and mental toil, and you are away to the mountains or to the sea for rest. Why are you going for rest? Why do you want rest? I ask. That I may regain my strength. For what?

Cross-examine yourself and see the meaning of your activity. Analyze your own wishing and desire, and see what inspiration lies at the back of it. If, by God's infinite grace and by the indwelling of the Holy Christ Himself, at the back of all the activity and of all desire and all speech, there is the perpetual aspiration, "Thy Kingdom come, thy will be done," then every act, every thought, is prayer.

"They ought always to pray, and not to faint." If we do not pray always, we never pray. The man who makes prayer a scheme by which occasionally he tries to get something for himself has not learned the deep, profound secret of prayer. Prayer is life passionately wanting, wishing, desiring God's triumph. Prayer is life striving and toiling everywhere and always for that ultimate victory. When men so pray they do not faint. They mount up with wings as eagles, they run without weariness, they tramp the hardest, roughest road, and they do not faint.

God-centered Praying

My desire has been to arrest irreverent and unintelligent prayer, to indicate a line of contrast which will reveal to all of us the fact that prayer is infinitely larger than we have often thought it to be. I charge upon you in this life of faith, do not degrade prayer to a low standard of experience, or make it that by which you attempt to gain things–and notice the startling language of Scripture–that you may spend them on your own lusts. "Ye have not because ye ask not," or "ye have not because ye ask amiss" (James 4:2-3). What is it to ask amiss? To ask for things that I may spend them on my own desires. That is praying that is not answered. Men "ought always to pray, and not to faint."

Oh, may I learn the lesson of Jesus that God is other than the unjust judge, that my method with Him may be other than that of the imploring widow, and that if I only know what prayer really is, I live at home in omnipotence, and I need never faint by the way. May this strength be ours.

How to Pray

Amzi Clarence Dixon (1854-1925) was a Baptist
preacher who ministered to several congregations
in the South before becoming pastor of the Moody
Memorial Church in Chicago (1906-11). He left
Chicago to pastor the famous Metropolitan
Tabernacle in London, "Spurgeon's Tabernacle"
(1911-19). He died in 1925 while pastoring the
University Baptist Church, Baltimore, Maryland.
A close associate of Reuben A. Torrey, Dixon
helped him edit *The Fundamentals*. Dixon was a
popular preacher in both Britain and America.
This sermon is from *Through Night To Morning*,
published 1913 by Robert Scott.

12

HOW TO PRAY

After this manner therefore pray ye (Matthew 6:9).

LUKE TELLS us that as Jesus was praying in a certain place, when He ceased, one of His disciples said unto Him, "Lord, teach us to pray." This disciple had heard Jesus preach, but he did not feel like saying, "Lord, teach us to preach." He could learn to preach by studying the methods of the Master. But there was something about the praying of Jesus which made the disciple feel that he did not know how to pray, that he had never prayed, and that he could not learn by listening even to the Master as He prayed.

There is a profound something about prayer which never lies on the surface. To learn it, one must go to the depths of the soul and climb to the heights of God. The importance of it cannot be overestimated. Luther's motto gives us the secret of success along all lines: "To have prayed well is to have studied well." To have prayed well is to have preached well, to have written well, to have worked well, to have resisted well, to have lived well, and to have died well. Prayer is the key to success. Not to pray is to fail. To pray aright is never to fail.

How infinitely important, then, that we should know how to pray, and Christ tells us how.

Pray Genuinely

"When thou prayest, thou shalt not be as the hypocrites" (Matthew 6:5). The word *hypocrite* means mainly just "a play actor." In prayer, do not act a part. It is not saying a form of words in a certain posture of body. Seriousness can be simulated; an actor can play a serious part. Earnestness can be simulated; an actor can play an earnest part. Even tears can be simulated, but there is no playing the part of genuineness. Make-believe genuineness is impossible, for genuineness has to do with the inner reality. Genuineness is character that God sees, and in it there is no acting a part before God. He sees through all pretence. In prayer be genuine, for you are dealing with God. Prayer is a personal transaction between the soul and God.

Pray Secretly

"When thou prayest, enter into the closet, and when thou hast shut the door, pray to thy Father in secret" (Matthew 6:6). "When thou prayest" means literally, "Whenever thou prayest." Let all thy praying be in thy closet with the door shut with everything and everybody shut out except God and you. "Pray to thy Father in secret," and then the answer will be no secret. It will be known that God answers prayer.

Does this mean that I shut myself up on some private room to pray? Yes, you can do that and ought to do it as often as possible. But entering a room and locking the door does not always mean mental privacy. A thousand things may follow and so occupy our attention that we shall not pray at all. Our form of words will be but an actor's part. Pretending to be occupied with God, we are really occupied with things that distract us. And in the presence of others, even of a great congregation, the public prayer may be so occupied with God as to be a personal, private transaction with Him. Even in the presence of others we may enter into the closet and shut the door to all distractions while we pray to "our Father in secret."

All real prayer is private with God the only auditor. The presence of the audience may suggest praise and petition, but the prayer is not a dealing with the audience at all, but only with God. In preaching we speak to the people for God, and in public prayer we speak to God for the people. Yet no real prayer is public in the consciousness of him who prays. The actor in prayer loves to stand praying in the synagogues, and on the street corners to "be seen of men." Jesus says, "They have their full reward" (Matthew 6:5). They will be seen of men, and that is all they will get. Men will call them very religious, and perhaps praise their prayers as eloquent, but God pays no attention to them.

Prayer may be public or private, but it must always be secret in the sense that it is a personal transaction between the soul and God. Even if a thousand people should join in the same prayer, only those would really pray who deal personally with God.There are no proxies in prayer. We pray *for* one another, but not *instead of* one another. I may intercede for you, but I cannot do your praying for you. To do so would be to curse rather than to bless you.

The meaning of the Greek word translated "closet" is very suggestive. It's primary meaning is "storehouse" or "barn," a place where valuables are kept. It is the word Jesus uses in Luke 12:24, when He speaks of the ravens not laying up in storehouse or barn. It is the word *storehouse* in the Septuagint of Deuteronomy 28:8: "The Lord shall command the blessing upon thee in thy storehouses." It is the word translated "barn" in Proverbs 3:10: "So shall thy barns be filled with plenty." The idea of secrecy came out of the fact that men usually store their valuables in a secret place, and the word came to mean an inner chamber, because the wealthy often had such a secret room in their houses for the storing of valuables. "When thou prayest," says Jesus, "enter thou into thy secret treasure chamber."

The place of real prayer is the Christian's treasure chamber. He is there in the midst of the treasures of grace which God has given him, and it is there that God enriches him more and more; but in the secret place of the Most High where He dwells, he is rich in love, joy, peace, and all the fruits of the Spirit.

Pray Definitely

"When ye pray, use not vain repetitions, as the heathen do; for they think that they shall be heard for their much speaking" (Matthew 6:7). "Use vain repetitions" is one word in the Greek, and means primarily "to stammer." The stammerer repeats his words in a meaningless way, and in prayer we are not to do that. God wants us to express our needs in a clear, intelligent manner. There is no merit to saying prayers over and over and counting our beads so as to keep account of the number of times. That is the way the heathen do, but Jesus says, "Be not like unto them." The heathen think they must gain their god's attention and make an impression upon him in behalf of their petitions. It is not so with our God, for He knows what we have need of before we ask Him. The asking is for our sakes so that our faith and love and hope may be exercised and strengthened.

Pray Fraternally

"Our Father." We have seen that real prayer, though public, is secret, in that it deals with God alone; and now it appears that even solitary prayer should be social. We are so united in family ties to all Christians that one of us cannot suffer without all suffering, and none of us can rejoice without all rejoicing. A blessing upon one is, therefore, a blessing upon all, and a curse upon one is a curse upon all. "I," "me," and "my" do not appear in this prayer; while "we," "us" and "our" occur nine times.

The phrase "in heaven" is worthy of our study. "In the heavens" is the literal translation. To the Jewish and Oriental mind there were three heavens. The first was the region of air and cloud where winds blow, thunder peals, and lightnings flash. The second heaven was the region of sun, moon, and stars—the sidereal heavens, vaster to our vision since the telescope was invented. The third heaven to which Paul was caught up, whether in the body or out of it he could not tell (2 Corinthians 12:2), was the region of God's throne and glory, the home of the angels.

Now, "Our Father" is in all these heavens He rules supreme. Astrologers taught that the stars ruled over the destinies of men. To be born under an evil star was a very bad omen; the moon struck people with madness.

"Our Father" is the God of the sun, moon, and stars. He is great enough to fill the infinitude of space. Because we are under His care, the sun shall not smite us by day, nor the moon by night. Sun, moon, and stars are obedient servants doing His will. "Our Father" also rules in the elements of air and clouds. There is a "Prince of the power of the air." He is a rebellious prince, usurping a portion of our Father's dominions, but we are not afraid of him.

Pray Reverently

"Hallowed be Thy name." Though children crying familiarly "Abba, Father," we must not forget to be reverent. The pious Jew had such reverence for the name of Jehovah that he never pronounced it. It lost its vowel points by disuse, so that Hebrew scholars differ today as to how it ought to be pronounced. Let no word pass our lips which in any way takes the name of God in vain.

Pray Loyally and Hopefully

"Thy kingdom come." Our Father is a King, and while we are permitted to be lovingly familiar, we must be loyally true. Disloyalty to the king is treason. The King came to earth and they rejected Him. The Church has its mission between the rejected King and the coming kingdom. At some time, perhaps soon, the King will return to set up His kingdom. It is our business to make ready for His return and welcome Him when He comes.

It is said of a great general that he expressed his purpose to destroy all his enemies, but when he had captured the opposing army, he forgave them and sent them home to their families. When asked why he did not keep his word, he replied, "I have destroyed all my enemies; they are now my friends." God would destroy all His enemies by making them His friends by the power of His forgiving love in Jesus Christ.

While we pray for the coming of the King in His glory, it is our duty and privilege to let Him come in His grace. Let us crown Him in the province of our hearts and lives. Christ must be enthroned in every department of my being–intellectual, moral, spiritual and physical. I would crown Him in the realm of religion, business, education, politics and pleasure.

Pray Submissively and Aggressively

"Thy will be done in earth, as it is in heaven." "Heaven" is here singular and evidently refers to the highest heaven, where God reigns in righteousness. In heaven the will of God is done perfectly and joyfully; there is no resistance. His will is law, and it is never violated. Such is the standard we should have before us, and we should be satisfied with nothing less. This spirit will make us foreign missionaries and send us with the Gospel to the uttermost parts of the earth. It will also make us home missionaries, sending us into the alleys and avenues wherever we can find a soul in rebellion against God.

Pray Dependently

"Give us this day our daily bread." "This day," of course, refers to time. But the word "daily," which occurs nowhere else in the New Testament, has in it no thought of time. It means "needed," "necessary." "Give us daily the food that is necessary for use, not only quantity, but also in quality." It is a prayer that we may have the wisdom to eat the right kind of food, in the right way, at the right time. More people are hurt by gormandizing than by fasting.

The worker can pray this prayer for a certain kind of food is necessary for the strengthening of his body for his manual toil. The writer, who sits at his desk, should pray this prayer, for he needs another kind of food for his nerves and brain. The millionaire can pray this prayer, for he needs wisdom that he may eat just the food he needs. While a certain millionaire was in poor health, it is said that he carried with him in his travels a specialist to tell him what proportion of milk and biscuits he should eat. His millions could furnish an abundance of food, but special wisdom was required as to quality and quantity.

This prayer is, therefore, as appropriate for the man with a large bank account as for the man who walks the street not knowing where his next meal is to come from. It is also a prayer for the housekeeper and the cook so that they may have skill and wisdom in selecting and preparing the food that is necessary for the family.

Pray Penitently

"Forgive us our debts, as we forgive our debtors." The word translated "debt" means "that which is justly or legally due." An overdue obligation is a sin. It is not a sin to borrow or give your note promising to pay at a certain time. We really "owe no man anything" until the time for payment has arrived. But the day an obligation becomes due we must pay it or ask forgiveness of the creditor.

Our sins against God are all debts overdue, and we are bankrupt. We owe ten thousand talents and have not a penny to pay. It is a debt to the justice of God, and the love of God in Jesus Christ makes full payment for all who will confess their sins and gratefully accept the payment.

Pray Cautiously

"Lead us not into temptation, but deliver us from the Evil One." We should make no spectacular display of courage. "A fence at the top of the precipice is better than a hospital at the bottom." We should keep as far from danger as possible. Better use our strength in doing good than in resisting evil. But if, with all our caution, we fall into the snare of the devil and are caught in the meshes of his wiles, there is One able to deliver. Call to Him and He will come to your rescue. He will make a way of escape.

Let us close where we began. "Lord, teach us to pray." The request is not *how* to pray, though; as we have seen, He does teach us how. Neither is it *what* to pray, though He does teach us *what*. We know *how* to pray and *what* to pray better than we pray. "Lord, teach us to PRAY." We are tempted to let other good things displace prayer. As a result, we spend hours, days, and weeks for other things but only minutes for prayer. Knowing how and what is not sufficient. We must take time to do it, for God works in answer to prayer, and God at work is our greatest need.

The Ladder of Prayer

George H. Morrison (1866-1928) assisted the great Alexander Whyte in Edinburgh, pastored two churches, and then became pastor in 1902 of the distinguished Wellington Church on University Avenue in Glasgow. His preaching drew great crowds; in fact, people had to queue up an hour before the services to be sure to get seats in the large auditorium. Morrison is a master of imagination in preaching; yet his messages are solidly biblical. From his many published volumes of sermons, I have chosen this message, found in *The Afterglow of God*, published 1912 by Hodder and Stoughton, London.

G.H. Morrison

13

THE LADDER OF PRAYER

Behold a ladder set up on the earth, and the top of it reached to heaven (Genesis 28:12).

THIS IS a remarkable verse about a memorable scene. Today in this sermon I wish to use the imagery of the verse without direct regard to its context. In some of our devotional writers we read of what is called the ladder of prayer. Prayer is regarded as the ascent to God, up which, step by step, the soul is borne. And these devotional writers, often with great power and penetration, dwell on the separate steps of the ascent that carry the heart upward to the throne. In other words, they show where prayer begins and to what heights it is capable of rising. They trace its stages, not by formal logic, but by the large experience of men. And it is on that ladder of prayer I should like to dwell, beginning with the lowest step and so ascending to the higher ones.

Step One – Emergency Prayer

Prayer, then, commonly begins with the cry of escape from some external evil. The lowest step on the ladder of the soul is the cry wrung from disaster or adversity. When a man is faced with a dangerous operation, when he finds himself (as in shipwreck) in dire peril, when someone who is very dear to him is ill, or in a situation of great hazard, I say that then there is an instinct of the heart which urges to a cry of help to God, and it is in such a cry that prayer is often born.

Now it is one sign of what I should venture to call the *humanity* of Holy Scripture that it preserves for us such a vast store of prayers of this initial kind. The Bible is the great record of the soul – please notice – and such prayers are *not* for blessings of the soul. They are wrung out, not in spiritual darkness, but in some kind of distress.

And yet the Bible is so superbly human in its handling of this life of ours that it is a very treasury of prayers which some would scarcely reckon prayers at all. It does not ignore them because they are untouched by the deep sense of spiritual alienation. The Bible does not rule such desperate prayers out of the soul's history because there is in them yet no plea for pardon. It knows our frame— remembers we are dust—and is touched like the Lord with the feeling of our infirmities. It welcomes the strong cry—and calls it prayer—that is uttered in adversity.

God's Great Patience

This, too, always seems to me to glorify the patience of our Lord. For I suppose that of every ten prayers men made to Jesus, not fewer than nine were of this kind. Of course, we cannot tell what the disciples asked for in their seasons of sweet and secret intercourse. "Teach us to pray" (Luke 11:1), "Show us the Father" (John 14:8)— such hints may move us at least to hope the best. But we *do* know that as Jesus moved about, and men drew near and cried to Him, nine times out of ten the things they cried for could scarcely be called spiritual at all. Some prayed for sight. They prayed for physical power. They prayed that a son or daughter might be healed. Others prayed in the wild uproar of the storm, "Lord, save us: we perish" (Matthew 8:25).

And what I say is that for one like Jesus, to whom the spiritual overshadowed everything, such ceaseless pray— ing for the physical and temporal must have made His cross heavier to bear. It deepens the wonder of His patience to remember that He accepted so many prayers of distress. It sheds a light on His infinite compassion. He certainly wanted to have been asked for deeper things; yet He never wearied in bestowing these things. And so may we learn that in the ear of God those cries, which are but the rudiments of prayer, are neither rejected nor despised.

Step Two—Confession

That, then, is the first step on the ladder, and now above it there is another step. It is the stage when prayer for outward help becomes a cry for deliverance from sin. In the first outbreak of appeal to heaven, there is scarcely any consciousness of sin. There is no thought of anything but the calamity which has befallen us or some one who is dear. But slowly, as a person prays for help, there steals on him the strange conviction that he needs something deeper than assistance and that in the sight of God he is a sinner.

It would lead us far beyond our bounds today to consider how the sense of sin is born. It is created by the Holy Spirit in ways that oftentimes defy analysis. Yet it, I think, is very largely true that when a man prays in trouble or adversity, gradually there is awakened in him the feeling that he is a sinner. I have heard people who have had to suffer greatly say, "What a sinner I must have been, when God has sent me this." Now of course, in the light of the words of Jesus, they were unwarranted in saying that. Still, it betrayed that lurking sense to which few, I take it, are quite strangers that when suffering falls on us or those we love, near the suffering is guilt.

I wonder if a father ever saw his child suffer without some dark suspicion of that kind. Childish pain not only excites pity; it has a strange way of getting at the conscience. When some one dear to us has to suffer greatly, and we begin to pray for them in secret, we find ourselves crying, ere we close, "God be merciful to me a sinner."

It is thus that prayer, in the ordering of God, rises to what is called the second stage. Born in the need of help in some dark hour, it passes onward to the need of pardon. It deepens into prayer for forgiveness, for the inward cleansing of the heart, and for deliverance, through the grace of God, from the sin that doth so easily beset us.

I want you here to note in passing how often Jesus sought to deepen prayer so. He took prayer by the hand—if I might put it thus—and led it upward to this higher step. People came to him and asked for something physical; Christ lent a willing ear to them and answered them. They asked for sight, and Jesus gave them sight; they asked for bodily health, and He bestowed it. But you know how often when He bestowed such gifts–when He answered the prayer for outward things like these–He turned the thought of the sufferer to *sin.* "Go," he would say to them, "and sin no more" (John 8:11). Was it merely a word of warning for the future? I do not think you exhaust the thought of Jesus when you narrow it in any way like that. He was leading men into that deeper life which can never be satisfied with outward blessings, but which feels, in the very bestowal of such benefits, the need of pardon and release from sin.

That, then, is the second step of prayer, and God, I think, brings most of us to that. We are no longer crying wildly heavenward, as in some shipwreck or calamity. We are crying for a clean heart and a right spirit; we are crying, "Against thee and thee only have we sinned", and to every such true cry is given the answer, "Though your sins be as scarlet, they shall be white as snow" (Isaiah 1:18).

Step Three–Supplication for God's Grace

Well, now we pass on to the third stage in the upward progress of the life of prayer, for we come to find that deliverance is not everything, if our walk is to be well-pleasing before God. Our Savior spoke of a house that was swept and garnished, and yet it became the dwelling-place of devils. If it was to be the home of light and love, it needed something more than cleansing. And so do men awaken, when they have prayed for pardon, to their abiding need of something more than pardon, if they are to be clothed in the comeliness of love. There are virtues that they must achieve. There are graces that they must attain. Patience is needed, and courage, and control, if they are to walk in the light as He is in the light.

And so prayer rises from the cry for pardon into the range and compass of petition and becomes the daily appeal of the endeavoring soul for needed virtue and for needed grace. It is true that our Father knows what things we need before one syllable of prayer has left the lip. But Christ, who told us of His knowledge, has told us also that the Father delights to have His children asking. And the fact is that in such holy mysteries there is little to be gained by argument; it is far wiser, in a childlike trust, to accept the perfect leadership of Jesus. "Ask, and it shall be given you; . . . knock, and it shall be opened unto you" (Matthew 7:7). We must *still* ask – we must *still* knock – though our Father knows the things of which we have need.

And hence it is that in the Christian life there is such a range of petitionary prayer, from the lowliest virtue that the weakest person needs, to the loftiest grace that can adorn the saint. We are a long way now from the wild cry that rises in some season of disaster. We are breathing a different, though not a diviner, air than in the moment when our one thought was pardon. We have risen into a life of need which is wide as the mercy and the grace of God, and that is the third step upon the ladder.

The First Steps – Involving Our Desires

Now if you will turn back in thought and survey the road that we have travelled, you will find that all the stages mentioned have at least one common element. What is that element? Well, it is this. It is the presence in them all of *self*. It is the stealing of self onto the scene in the solemn moment of approach to God. Notice that I do not say such prayers are selfish. To say that would be to misinterpret everything. A man is *not* selfish because he prays for healing or because he asks God for some special grace. All I say is that in these prayer-stages, sometimes with far more insistence than at other times, there is felt, in every approach to God, the presence, if not the pressure, of the self.

Now the question is: Is there any prayer possible where self shall be utterly forgotten? Is there any prayer where the very thought of self would be lost and hidden and absorbed in God? If there is such, then prayer is at its highest, and we have reached the topmost step upon the ladder, which rises from the Bethel where we rest and reaches to the glory of the throne.

Step Four – Real Submission to God's Will

The answer is that such prayer is not only possible, but is within the grasp of everyone of us. It is born when a man has learned to look to God and to say with his whole heart, "Thy will be done." There is no longer any thought of *our* will; our will is merged in the sweet will of God. Through light and shadow, gladness and adversity, the perfect will of God is being wrought. And so each day, not choosing for ourselves, we take what God in His infinite wisdom sends us, and our life becomes a prayer, "Thy will be done." We do not ask to see the distant scene now. We do not blindly insist on *this* or *that*. We do not complain when blessings are denied us or because there is sorrow where we had looked for joy. We have ceased to think that we know what we most need. We have ceased to think we can direct our steps. Through all that is sent to us and all we have to do, our one prayer is, "Thy will be done."

There may be many a struggle before that stage is reached. There was struggle for Jesus before that stage was reached – "If it be possible, let this cup pass from me; nevertheless not as I will, but as Thou wilt" (Matthew 26:39). But *when* it is reached, then there is perfect peace and a new light on everything that happens; and self, which even in our petitions vexed us, passes in music out of sight. *That* is the highest reach of prayer when it is grasped in the fulness of its meaning. That is something nobler than petition. It is communion with the Father of all spirits. It is the voicing of the passion to obey whether obedience be hard or pleasant, and without obedience there can be no religion.

The Beginning of Joy and Power in Prayer

In closing, let me make two remarks on the last and highest stage in prayer. The first is that it is at this stage that joy in prayer commonly begins. There are many who pray, and pray with regularity, who have never experienced joy in prayer. They hold to the practice from a sense of duty, but it is a duty to which they have to force themselves. Knowing how surely the omission of secret prayer leads to unguardedness and unbelief, they cling to it in the dark with fine fidelity.

Now it would take me far beyond my theme to discuss generally the lack of joy in prayer. But perhaps the commonest of all causes of that absence is to be found along the lines I have been indicating.

I question if there is ever joy in prayer when men come to the Father wanting their *own* way. That joy is born when they have learned to come wanting nothing but the way of God. It is then that there comes sweet peace into the soul. It is then that we learn that no evil can befall us. It is then that we find, through fair and foul, that underneath are the everlasting arms. And this is such a wonderful discovery, in a life so difficult and intricate as ours, that it brings the ransomed of the Lord to Zion with songs and everlasting joy upon their heads.

And the other remark which I would make is that we owe it to Christ that all of us can pray so. It is Christ who has made it possible even for the weakest to reach this highest stage of prayer. If God were an unknown ruler in the distance, only a hero could pray, "Thy will be done." If He were but a Spirit of omnipotence, such prayer would take far stronger faith than ours. But Christ has taught us that God is our Heavenly Father, and that He loves us with a perfect love, and that the very hairs of our head are numbered, and that He does not will that any one soul should perish. Given a character of God like *that,* it is not impossible to pray, "Thy will be done."

We pray in the childlike and Christ-given confidence that in the will of God there is our highest good. And there we leave it, not seeing what it means perhaps, for now we know in part and see in part; but we are quietly certain that the day is coming when we shall say, "He has done all things well."

When I Find It Hard To Pray

William E. Sangster (1900-1960) was the "John Wesley" of his generation as he devoted his life to evangelism and the promotion of practical sanctification. He pastored in England and Wales, and his preaching ability attracted the attention of the Methodist leaders. He ministered during World War II at Westminister Central Hall, London, where he pastored the church, managed an air-raid shelter in the basement, and studied for his Ph.D. at the London University! He served as president of the Methodist Conference (1950) and director of the denomination's home missions and evangelism ministry. He published several books on preaching, sanctification, and evangelism, as well as volumes of sermons. This message comes from *He is Able*, published in 1936 by Hodder and Stoughton, London.

W.E. Sangster

14

WHEN I FIND IT HARD TO PRAY

ONE DAY a university student came to see me on the matter of prayer. He reminded me of an address which I had given and asked whether he had understood me aright that John Henry Newman and Andrew Bonar both gave two hours a day to prayer. I said he had heard me correctly. I went on to say that there was nothing singular about that so far as the saints were concerned and talked to him of the devotional habits of other people who hungered and thirsted after righteousness and how, despite their exceedingly busy lives, they spent many hours in prayer.

His bewilderment grew. "What beats me," he said, "is how they filled up the time. It is hard to imagine how men with many duties to do could give the amount of time to it, but it is still harder to know how they used it, once it was set aside. I can't pray for ten minutes. I've tried. I kneel down every night and just ask God to forgive me for anything I've done wrong. I thank Him for His blessings. I mention mother and father and my other relations. I say a word about my friends, and the church, and then I'm done. Sometimes I stay a bit longer, but my mind keeps going off at a tangent, and I've nothing more to say. Five minutes covers it. How people can pray for two hours beats me."

The perplexity of that young man is a very common one. It is not to be confused with doubts about the theory and efficacy of prayer; it is a matter of method and prac-tice. Many people who have no difficulty about the duty and value of devotion and who are not barring their own way by deliberate indulgence in known sin fail in the *act* of prayer. Some who have been Christians for years are still in the kindergarten of this school and, seeing that prayer is the very heart of the devotional life, their spiritual progress clearly depends on learning how to pray. In the days of His flesh, His disciples said, "Lord teach us to pray."

He is able to teach us still.

The Obstacle of Time

The obstacles to prayer are many, though some are mere excuses and would quickly yield to a resolute act of will. There is the difficulty about time. People complain that their busy lives give them no time for prayer, but it is usually a shallow evasion because they clearly find time for less important things—the newspaper and amusements. No one deeply in love would fail to find time for a daily word with the loved one, if the loved one lived at hand. Christ stole time from His sleep to pray. Wesley rose every morning at 4 a.m. for the same purpose. Francis Asbury was astir at five.

The first thing in the morning is the best time for prayer, but if peculiar circumstances really make that impossible, the keen mind will find time before the day is old. One of the busiest women I have ever known, a working-class woman with a large family, keeps her tryst with God in the early afternoon when the last member of the family has returned from the midday meal. Before beginning again, she reads the Book of God and spends time in unhurried prayer. "Then," she says, "I wire in again."

It is not always possible for a will to find a way, but it *is* possible in the matter of prayer. Time *can* be found. One could begin with a minimum rule of fifteen minutes each day. Even so slight an investment of well-used time would bring a vast and precious gain.

The Obstacle of Place

Then there is the difficulty about place. If it is possible, it is glorious to have a little oratory in the home, some private spot kept for devotions and marked by a sacred picture or symbol. Such a spot gathers associations and calls us to prayer even when inclination ebbs.

But that is not always possible. In overcrowded homes privacy is hard to find, and people complain that this prevents them from praying. It need not. Let them start earlier for work and slip into a church and pray there. And let them strive to build an oratory within their heart, a sacred silence inside them, to which they can retreat in the midst of noise and chatter. It is astonishing how real a secret chamber can be built within the heart by imagination and consecrated thought. In an over-crowded room, in a bus or train or tram, the mind can learn by practice how to be deaf to all distractions and climb the hidden stair to the sacred place: a chapel, a quiet room, a garden, howsoever one has pictured it, but where Jesus abides and greets you with a smile and says, "You have come." The saints have long known the secret.

Nor should it be forgotten by those whose prayers are hindered by the lack of privacy that it is always possible to go for a walk with Jesus. What conversation one can have with Christ on a lonely walk! Who does not know of the walk that Alexander Whyte had with God during his Christmas holiday at Bonskeid, "the best strength, and the best sweetness of all my Christmas holiday?" And how, after eight cold miles, he saw at last Schiehallion clothed in white from top to bottom, and poured out his soul as David did: "Wash me, and I shall be whiter than snow" (Psalm 5:7). Who does not remember how he walked back under the rising moon with his heart in a flame of prayer?

> Where'er we seek Thee Thou art found,
> And every place is hallowed ground.

The Obstacle of Tiredness

Some people complain that they are too weary to pray. Enquiry shows that this excuse is made by those who leave their prayer to the end of a tired day. It is both irreverent and unprofitable, to treat our devotions in such a fashion. The majority of us come to our beds heavy with fatigue, and some final act of committal is the most we are capable of. "Into Thy hands, O Lord, I commend my spirit." If our serious prayer is all left till then, it is small wonder if we find it a burden and fall asleep as we pray.

"Rabbi" Duncan, at one time professor of Hebrew in New College, Edinburgh, and a man of vast learning in the Oriental tongues, was suspected by his students of offering his private prayers in Hebrew. It is said that two of them determined to prove the truth or falsity of this rumor by listening outside his bedroom door just after he had retired for the night. Everything went according to plan. They heard the old scholar putter about his room for some minutes and then kneel to pray. But it was no Hebrew that came. The erudite old saint just said:

> Gentle Jesus, meek and mild,
> Look upon a little child,
> Pity my simplicity,
> Suffer me to come to Thee. Amen!

That was all. His deep prayer had been offered earlier in the day with a fresh mind. He committed himself to God at the last with the simple words of childhood. The listeners heard the bed creak and knew that "Rabbi" Duncan had gone to sleep. Reverence, as well as the simple sense of the thing, demands that we pray before we are too weary to pray well.

Mental Obstacles

Lack of imagination and an undisciplined mind are also obstacles to prayer. Building a chapel in the soul, for which we have pleaded, seems impossible to people deficient in imagination, and, if imagination built it, their inability to concentrate would make it difficult for them to worship there. The great Bishop Butler certainly assumed "a license in the use of words" when he derided imagination. It is a great gift of God to men. Modern psychology is emphathic on the point. To see the unseen by an effort of the mind, to look at Jesus, to be present (as Ruskin said) "as if in the body, at every recorded event in

the history of the Redeemer"—this gives a wing to earth-
born creatures and scales the heights of heaven.

What need there is to exercise imagination in prayer!
The person who feels that he is merely speaking into
space soon ceases to speak at all. The person who both
reads his Bible and prays with imagination finds that the
book becomes autobiographical and that his prayers produce a deep delight.

It is a sanctified imagination which would revolution-
ize the devotions of many people. If they lived *in* the
Gospels and felt themselves to be the leper whom Jesus
healed, the blind man whose sight He restored, the dying
thief whom He pardoned, the disciples who first heard
that He had risen from the dead, what a delight the book
would become! And if they turned in that spirit to prayer
and *saw* Him, how swiftly the prayer would flow. The
Psalmist said, "I have set the Lord always before me." So
can the simplest soul. Imagination was given to us that
while yet on earth, we might mingle with the heavenly
throng. We close our eyes in prayer that we might open
them to glory. Let us *see* God, and prayer will break from
us as the water gushed from the rock.

Lady Tennyson had a lovely face. Even the scornful
housemaid who contemptuously referred to her master,
the poet, as "only a public writer," said of her mistress,
"Oh, she is an angel." Tennyson himself remarked one
night to a friend, after his wife had gone to bed, "It is a
tender, spiritual face." Her looks matched her spirit, and
her sanctity was outstanding even in an age of formal
goodness. She knew the use of imagination in prayer.
She told her husband once: "When I pray, I see the face of
God smiling upon me."

Let no beginner in prayer abandon the privilege because of mind wandering. It can be conquered. A brisk,
live imagination and a resolute will cannot be denied.
Even though, in the early stages, the precious minutes
tick away and all the time seems spent in bringing the
mind back from its wanderings and fixing it again on
prayer, they are not moments lost. Such discipline will
exercise the muscles of the will, and the day will dawn

when the sweetest meditation and the most earnest prayer will be possible even amid distraction.

Emotions as Obstacles

Enslavement to feeling is another fruitful cause of neglected prayer. People do not pray because they do not feel like it, and they offer the excuse with a certain cheerful assurance that it will be accepted. They assume that prayers are only efficacious when they rise from an eager and emotional heart.

Nothing could be further from the truth. Many of the saints believe that floods of feeling belong only to the elementary stages of discipleship. All of them agree that we must keep our appointments with God, whether we feel like it or not. The most noble and enjoyable vocations bring their times of drudgery. If life was lived on a basis of feeling alone, nothing would be stable; appointments would not be kept; morality would be undermined; caprice would dethrone order in this world. If we have an engagement with a friend at a certain hour, we keep it, however disinclined we may feel when the time comes. Are we to be less courteous with God?

Nor should it be forgotten that God can do more for us when we pray against inclination than when we pray with it. The meek submission of our will deepens our surrender; our resolution to engage in prayer strengthens thought control. We rise from such prayers infinitely stronger than if we had knelt only at the dictate of desire. Faith, not feeling, measures the efficacy of prayer. Jesus never said, "Thy feeling hath made thee whole." He put the emphasis always on faith, and faith receives a finer witness when we pray against inclination than when we pray with it.

The Obstacle of Silence

Too much stress upon speaking is the final common obstacle that we will mention. People unpracticed in prayer suppose that no prayer is being offered unless they are talking all the time. They seem to know nothing of quiet adoration or the silent rapture of gazing on those glorious scars. Augustine said that our prayers ought to contain not *multa locutio* but *multa precatio*—"not much speaking, but much prayer." The method of prayer taught by Studdert Kennedy was largely wordless. It depended on lifting pictures, by a devout imagination, from the gospels and gazing and gazing on them. None who has practiced it will deny its power. To join the company in the upper room and have one's feet washed by Jesus is an awesome experience blasting the pride in our soul as by a great explosive.

There are times when speed is easy and when one can pour out the heart to God in a torrent of words, with all the natural simplicity of a child talking to his father, but never let it be thought that prayer is only for the fluent. God forbid! The most inarticulate can pray. When grief or disappointment or sin strikes one dumb, devotion does not end. There is still the upward look. Even when one weeps, it is one thing to weep to oneself and another to weep to Christ.

All the world knows now of old Père Chaffangeon, who used to remain for hours before the altar in the church at Ars without even moving his lips; it seems that he was speaking to God.

"And what do you say to Him?" the Curé asked.

"Oh," replied the old peasant, "He looks at me, and I look at Him."

"The greatest of mystics," says Henri Ghéon "have found no formula more simple, more exact, more complete, more sublime, to express the conversation of the soul with God."

Christ's Help for Prayer

But let us turn from the obstacles, and our simple counsel on how they may be overcome, to the help which Christ offers; so that the impulse to pray is nourished and the duty lost in the delight. A few minutes spent with the Bible is usually a swift preparation for prayer. A short, unhurried meditation on some fragment of Scripture and then silence quickens the spirit of devotion. George Müller of Bristol always approached his mighty prayers in that way and claimed that it delivered him from mind-wandering.

Prayer's Variety

Then think of the many aspects of prayer. The people who find their times of communion tedious often regard prayer as nothing more than asking for things. The many-sided nature of the devotional life is strange to them. There is *adoration*, the awesome, humbling obeisance of the self before God, and rapt gazing on glory when the soul soars "and time and sense seem all no more."

There is *confession*, which is not some trite phrase which bundles all our beastliness together and skates lightly away, saying, "Forgive me for anything I have done wrong." But confession involves a mind which pursues holiness with method, digs out the evil things inside us, and in the pure presence of God, looks and loathes.

There is *intercession*. How any man with faith in prayer and a heart to pity can fail to fill an odd half-hour at any time in earnest intercession is hard to understand. The burdens of mankind are so numerous and heavy that those who do not intercede lack either faith in prayer or feeling for their fellows.

There is *thanksgiving*, too. Addison declared that eternity was too short to utter all the gratitude of his heart, but most people leave it out entirely or dismiss it with a word. Is it hard for you to pray for ten minutes? In ten minutes one could hardly think of all the things which demand thanksgiving, much less include all the other aspects of prayer!

And if we leave petitions aside—and petitions can always look after themselves—there is still *consecration*, the fresh surrender of all the heart to God. "That vow renewed shall daily hear." What joy it is to gather every wandering thought and put one's whole life on the altar. What inward rest it is to feel the wonder of acceptance anew.

And all these are only *some* of the aspects of prayer. A wider survey of the country to be covered would surely serve the folk who find a sparsity of thought when they pray.

Prayer's Power

Not only is prayer quickened as we dwell on its many-sidedness but, still more, as we dwell upon its efficacy. Think of what it does. It changes the most intractable stuff in the universe—human nature—and makes sinners into saints. It brings heaven to earth. It fights vice and fosters virtue. It rescues souls in peril and becomes a password at the gate of death.

Prayer puts the sick and the infirm in the forefront of those who fight the battle of God. No one has ceased to serve who thinks to pray. It will dampen the delights of heaven for some of us when we discover how much prayer did on earth and remember that we prayed so little. A wounded soldier told me during the war that his convalescence at home had had one great pain for him. He witnessed his mother's anxiety for his brothers who were still at the front. He heard her prayers and saw her feverish anxiety concerning the letter carrier. He saw the furrows deepen in her face when neither letter nor field card was put in her hand. "It made me think," he said, "how often I might have written myself when I was out there, but thoughtlessly put it off." The memory of his selfishness was a shadow on the joys of home.

The memory of our prayerlessness may be a shadow on the joys of heaven. It may be that the greatest thing which we can do for anybody is to pray for them.

If a man treasures up the singular answers to prayer which he had heard, if he practices prayer and has his own answers to treasure up with them, he will not lapse into doubt. The experiment will end in an experience. There are many, many theoretical difficulties about prayer, but they are only academic questions to the people who pray. They *know* that it works and is real. They know.